D0593269

THE ECONOMICS OF DISTURBANCE

THE MACMILLAN COMPANY
NEW YORK · BOSTON · CHICAGO · DALLAS
ATLANTA · SAN FRANCISCO

MACMILLAN AND CO., LIMITED
LONDON · BOMBAY · CALCUTTA · MADRAS
MELBOURNE

THE MACMILLAN COMPANY
OF CANADA, LIMITED
TORONTO

THE ECONOMICS
OF DISTURBANCE

DAVID McCORD WRIGHT
Professor of Economics and Lecturer in Law, University of Virginia

1947

THE MACMILLAN COMPANY · NEW YORK

PALMER LIBRARY
CONNECTICUT COLLEGE

Copyright, 1946, by David McCord Wright

All rights reserved—no part of this book may be re-
produced in any form without permission in writing
from the publisher, except by a reviewer who wishes
to quote brief passages in connection with a review
written for inclusion in magazine or newspaper.

Printed in the United States of America

338.54
W931

*To the Planners of the
Future*

138861

FOREWORD

The basic theme of this study is the belief that our scattered and heterogeneous theories of economic disturbance may be grouped into a single generalized mode of statement whose key is the problem of orderly growth. The aim is not so much to spin novel theories as to effect a coherent synthesis and to impart a new emphasis to materials already at hand. A second major contention is the idea that the fundamental problems of disturbance are often matters of *value* rather than organization. In other words, given a certain set of values, it may sometimes prove impossible to eliminate sources of disturbance by changing social structure. Under appropriate circumstances, the values themselves imply the disturbance and social reorganization becomes a secondary though always important factor.

Because brevity has been sought, no attempt will be made to detail well known aspects of the problem as "hoarding" and the cumulative process of expansion and contraction. Anyone familiar with current controversy can fill in such gaps for himself without difficulty. Attention will be focused instead upon a group of problems submitted to be equally fundamental but unfortunately often slurred over at the present time.

Our emphasis will be placed primarily on diagnosis. We will not so much be looking for detailed answers to questions as pointing out the questions themselves, and indicating possible alternative lines of approach. We can scarcely be confident of curing a patient unless we have a fairly clear idea of what his disease may be. And it is precisely the necessary set of clear ideas which seem to the writer most lacking today. It is hoped that these insights of a "literary" economist will serve as an incentive and possible blueprint for further mathematical and statistical work. This book is a cross-country reconnoitering expedition. If we do not stay long at any one point, it is because our desire is most of all to get the general lay of the land.

Detailed acknowledgment of the many friends who have contributed to this book would be impossible. The influence of my Harvard teachers—especially Professors Schumpeter, Haberler, and Hansen will be immediately apparent. My debt to Professor Frank Knight of Chicago is equally clear. I wish, however, to render specific thanks to Professor D. H. Robertson of Cambridge, Professor Seymour Harris of Harvard, Professor Albert Gailord Hart of Columbia, and Professor Rutledge Vining of the University of Virginia, all of whom read the original manuscript and made many valuable suggestions. None of these gentlemen, of course, is to be held responsible for the views and the shortcomings of the final version. For those interested in such matters I should explain that the original draft was begun in 1941, and final revision made in the spring of 1946.

David McCord Wright

CONTENTS

CHAPTER I

BASIC MODEL AND ASSUMPTIONS

An economic system is not a lifeless aggregation of mechanical pulls. It is a process, a change, a becoming. It may be best compared to a living human body. As with the body, individual parts are not sharply separated but flow into one another, and, also as with the body, it is essential to healthy and efficient operation that the relative size of the various sections of the whole change with the stages of growth. In this problem of harmonious and symmetrical development—so familiar alike to the athlete and the philosopher—we find the kernel of any theory of disturbance. A child is born with organs and glands shaped with reference to the womb. As it grows these organs and glands begin to change. Some of them disappear altogether. At each point of development the relative proportions of the body will be altered. Failure of adjustment results in weakness, disease or death. So it is with an economic system.

Our first undertaking must therefore be to outline the chief divisions of the economic body whose relationship will help most in understanding social disturbance. But unfortunately a clear, functional, outline of the economic anatomy, is not easily attained. The units in which economists have usually thought— the "firm" or the "industry"—while useful for many purposes, are not sufficient in this connection. Furthermore, they inevitably tend to tie us down to certain capitalist restrictions. We must accordingly seek out a different classification.

One way of attempting such an outline would be to try, from the beginning, to find lines of separation applicable to all the multitudinous phenomena of the everyday world. This would plunge us at once into tremendous problems of definition from which we might never emerge. We might try, for example, to decide whether or not the Washington Monument was a "capital good," or ask whether, if training men in engineering be called "capital" goods production, what should be considered the role of training them in English literature? [1] An alternative approach, and the one to be adopted here, consists of setting up an initial model embodying the basic elements of the problem and then adding the necessary qualifications and elaborations in later chapters as the argument proceeds. By this method the fundamental concepts can be grasped at once without losing our way in a forest of detail.

A First Model

We commence by considering a single completely isolated economy having the following characteristics: (1) a labor force variously remunerated according to the distributive notions of its particular culture; (2) a huge circulating mass of intermediate goods, of various degrees of specialization, but all possessing the following attributes: (a) they are not produced or used for their own sake but only for further production; (b) they are all, in a very special sense, non durable—that is to say, many of them may be capable of storage for greater or less intervals but none of them can be used for purposes for which they are intended—i.e., for production—without disappearing or completely losing their form; (c) these intermediate commodities are all in the process of being made up into (3) durable "tools" by which will be meant all things useful in the production of yet further goods, which do not wear out or lose their form immediately upon use; or (4) non durable consumer's goods—things desired for their own sake, which, for purposes of our initial model, and solely for simplification, are supposed capable of storage but obliged to perish in yielding the sensory stimulation they were created to supply. In J. R. Hicks' term they are "single use" goods. You can put your cake on the shelf but you cannot eat it and have it, too.

1 Cf., the discussion in Chapter IV.

Looking at this society as a unit, we may conceive of all the "tools" in it as composing one vast machine for the production of consumer's goods or, more fundamentally, for the eventual presentation of certain stimuli to the minds and bodies of the population. For brevity's sake we may call this the "Great Machine."

If this Great Machine were unchanging and everlasting, the process of production would resemble the shovelling of coal into a furnace, or the operation of a stamping mill. Some laborers would feed in raw materials, others would operate the machine, while a third group would receive the finished product, and allocate it among the whole population according to the standards of their time and place. While the proportion of men actually engaged in putting the finishing touches to consumer's goods, or in distributing them, might be very small, the entire labor force could be considered as consumer's goods makers.[2] Since the equipment of society neither changed nor wore out, all productive energy would be directed toward one end—the production of consumer's goods and services, and no other activity would be needed.

But in the real world the Great Machine is neither immutable or eternal and the labor force is not composed solely of makers of consumer's goods. Instead we must add those men who are busied in maintaining, expanding, and changing the machine. These we will call the "tool makers"—the creators of new instruments of production. Such a simplified two-fold division naturally contains certain paradoxes and limitations. For example, since economic life is essentially circular, it follows that all the consumer's goods makers could be considered as tool makers and vice versa. For without consumer's goods the tool makers could not live, and without tools the makers of consumer's goods could not produce. However, we may validly draw the line at consumption—

[2] However, I agree with Professor Frank Knight that the training of a man is the preparation of a "capital good" or "tool." Thus even in our abstract model some people would have to be training the labor force and they would be "tool makers."

the satisfaction of the personal wants and desires of the population—and thus avoid complete circularity.

A much more substantial obstacle is presented by the usual
impossibility of identifying any one productive unit exclusively
with either of our two groups. A steel mill, for example, might
simultaneously be turning out steel for perishable toys and steel
for machinery. Similar difficulty is presented by the workers
handling and processing the vast mass of inventories and semi-
finished materials which is constantly moving through the system. Some of these "goods in process" may be identifiable from
the start as destined largely for consumption—wheat for example—but the majority are not so specific. Furthermore there
are also "loops" and "whirlpools" in the flow of materials. We
may, however, solve these problems analytically by one and the
same method. We may classify the workers in each industry
according to the proportion of their output appearing as tools
or as consumer's goods. In this way, though not without difficulty, we adhere to our twofold division of the labor force.

The next step in the construction of our model is to obtain
a clear idea of the interrelationship of the tool makers and the
makers of consumer's goods. The tool makers may be thought
of as producing a certain proportion of the raw materials of
society and from them manufacturing an unceasing flow of tools
which they turn over to the makers of consumer's goods. These,
in turn, with the aid of the tools thus delivered, are able to
make consumer's goods for the entire economy. On a primitive
island, for example, the tool makers might make boats and nets
which the makers of consumer's goods would use to catch fish.

It should be remembered, however, that in practically any
society, not all the tools produced are consumer's goods tools,
i.e., tools used by the makers of consumer's goods. We must
not forget the existence of the "machines which make the
machines." In our primitive island, for example, the boat
makers would undoubtedly have to make certain implements
to help them in their work and thus not all their efforts would
be spent on boats. A very large number of "tools" are used to

make still further tools. But while this modification introduces an important complicating factor of great importance in the analysis of disturbance, the fundamental relationships are not altered thereby. We still have two groups—makers of tools and makers of consumer's goods—and the first group is still *ultimately* concerned in making tools for the second. The fact that the tool makers take considerable time off in fashioning equipment for their own jobs does not affect the primary point.

The essentials of our model are given in Figure I, A. Triangular strips radiating from the left represent the flow of intermediate products which are being processed through the joint action of tools and labor. Vertical bars at the right of the triangle represent the final output of tools and consumer's goods. A horizontal line divides both final output and intermediate goods into the "tool making" and "consumer's goods making" groups. Broken lines are used to show that the final output of tools is distributed, upon completion, throughout all stages of manufactures in both sections of the economy. Solid lines show that consumer's goods are similarly passed back to workers throughout the entire system. We thus achieve a synthetic approximation of the whole real process of production.

With the addition of a few further assumptions our diagram may also be used to show the rudimentary relationships between real production and money income flow. We have assumed that the only durable goods in our model are instrumental goods or tools. All other products are either non-durable or "single use" goods. We may add to this the statement that our society is in full employment equilibrium and that inventories throughout the system are maintained always at the same figure. Assume further that all money "saved" is used to purchase tools; and all money "spent" to buy consumer's goods. These assumptions greatly simplify the task of indicating the role of saving, and this is done in Figure I, B. A single vertical strip represents the total final money income paid out per period. Under our assumptions such income is usually taken as exactly equal in value to total final output and is so drawn. Solid lines

FIGURE I

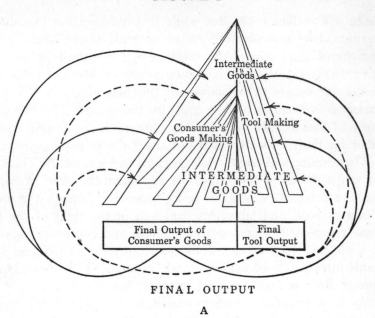

Intermediate
Goods

Consumer's
Goods Making

Tool Making

I N T E R M E D I A T E
G O O D S

| Final Output of Consumer's Goods | Final Tool Output |

FINAL OUTPUT

A

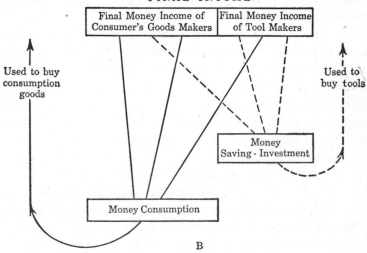

FINAL INCOME

| Final Money Income of Consumer's Goods Makers | Final Money Income of Tool Makers |

Used to buy
consumption
goods

Used to
buy tools

Money
Saving - Investment

Money Consumption

B

Note: It is not assumed or shown that all intermediate goods pass through all "stages" of the "triangle."

6

indicate that the amount of spending from total final money income just equals the value of current consumer's goods output. Similarly, broken lines show that individuals throughout the system save from final income an amount just equal in value to the current output of tools. It must be pointed out however, that just as in Figure IA a "triangle" of intermediate goods is shown behind final real output, so in IB a similar "triangle" of transactions balances should be drawn behind final money income and also that the monetary "triangle" would have to allow for, or abstract from, numerous loops and whirlpools in the flow.[3]

[3] Cf., E. F. M. Durbin, *The Problem of Credit Policy* (New York, J. Wiley & Sons, Inc., 1935), p. 36, Fig. 4.

CHAPTER II

SECULAR MONETARY FRICTIONS OF GROWTH

It might appear that in the preceding chapter we have done no more than outline, very abstractly, certain quite obvious relationships. In fact we have done a good deal more than that. For the diagrams of Chapter I imply no basic assumptions other than the use of tools and money, and such assumptions are not very restrictive. Yet broadly applicable though Figure I may be, two fundamental problems clearly emerge from it. First: What in real terms is the ideal relationship between the "tool making" and the "consumer's goods making" groups—in effect (in the model of Chapter I) what is the socially desirable real relationship between spending and saving? Next: How can the flow of money function smoothly in the real world? We shall begin with some aspects of the money problem.

Any developed modern socialism will almost inevitably use money. While the importance of money as a medium of exchange and store of value may be reduced, its function as a standard of value will be much greater. For the writer submits, and Russian experience verifies, that planning would be well nigh impossible without accounting and statistics. Yet if accounts are kept—especially capital accounts—and if decisions are based upon them—even if only partially—unexpected changes in the price level and in the value of money are potential sources of considerable difficulty. It follows that in considering secular monetary frictions of growth we are not limiting ourselves to purely capitalist phenomena, and that our results will have relevance for other societies as well.

Fashionable modern emphasis has placed attention almost

exclusively upon difficulties due to "hoarding," and liquidity preference, and these have been viewed primarily as the result of capitalist acquisitive motives. As a consequence, many socialist writers have been led to maintain that the abolition of capitalism would mean the end of hoarding which in turn would mean the removal of virtually all monetary difficulties. But such a view appears highly questionable. Even on its own terms there would still remain a price level problem, and there are related expenditure-price distortions which have no close connection with the usual hoarding analysis.

Unfortunately the elucidation of such problems is a rather cumbersome undertaking and many readers find detailed numerical sequence analysis very tedious. In order, therefore, to maintain proper balance of emphasis, we shall briefly summarize the conclusions of the present chapter at the beginning and those who wish to take them on trust may go forward to Chapter III without reading the supporting argument. The writer will not, however, disguise his personal opinion that those who have never worked through *quantitatively* the rudimentary relations between money saving, investment, expansion and the price level are unlikely to have a really clear idea of the nature and difficulty of the problem. The puzzle may be pieced together from various well known treatments in the modern literature. Nevertheless it is submitted that there is no single statement which is both sufficiently accurate and adequately comprehensive. Many important questions were obscured in the avalanche of the Keynesian revolution and in the long run I do not believe that the labor of disinterring and explaining some of them will be found futile.

The problem here concerning us is well summed up in the customary reference to the "money value of the supply of all goods" as "identical" with the "total money income earned in their production," or, again in Lord Keynes' remark that it is "indubitable . . . that the income derived in the aggregate by all the elements in the community concerned in a productive activity necessarily has a *value* exactly equal to the value of the output." [1] There are unquestionably senses in which such statements are indubitable—but are they the most relevant senses? If we substitute for the "money value of the supply of all goods" the expression "prices normally set *ex ante* by producers," and for "income earned in their production" the "current payment to consumers of final disposable money income," is there a uniquely necessary universal short run identity? A large body of dissenters has always answered "no," and an analysis of their views will be of the utmost assistance in developing our own conclusions.

Let us first of all make our terms clear. The frictions which we shall be investigating here need not be associated with any changes in velocity whatever. Next, monetary income-price difficulties may be identified with anticipatory price *increases* or the charging of "too high" a price. Such a view can always be rendered correct "by definition" since any price which does not clear the market can be called too high. But we are not talking here "by definition." The question is: Would a capitalist entrepreneur, or a socialist state productive unit, setting the price *ex ante* upon an increment of newly produced goods, in accordance with the best accounting practice, *necessarily* find disbursed sufficient current money income to meet that price? In other words we are discussing not hoarding but the possible disappointment of "reasonable" or "institutionally normal" expectations.

Roughly speaking, two views may be distinguished, both of which the author believes to be incorrect. First one finds writers who deny that any spontaneous equality of *ex ante* prices and current disposable income *ever* exists.[2] Next there are those who say it *always* exists. Though Lord Keynes himself, except in the case of "hoarding," has been as dogmatic as any in this connection, the writer submits that the solution to the problem closely

[1] J. M. Keynes, *The General Theory of Employment Interest and Money* (New York, Harcourt, Brace & Company, 1936), p. 20.

[2] I would have thought this the contention of Major Douglas and Foster and Catchings but there are times in which some social creditors, as well as Foster and Catchings, admit the exception of the stationary state.

resembles the Keynesian attitude toward unemployment. Just as we now know that full employment equilibrium, so long taken as "obviously" the only possible case, is but a special instance among many possibilities, so also the work of Professor Robertson, Mr. Durbin, Gaitskell and others shows clearly that the usual statement of the relationship of *ex ante* prices to income is likewise, in many important sense, a special case,[3] and does not hold good universally.

Throughout the present study the word growth will nearly always be more important than the word "socialism" or "capitalism." Possibly the mere institution of private property "automatically" gives rise to invention and expansion. But such an opinion is highly debatable and to settle it would lead us far afield. *Prima facic* a stationary society is perfectly compatible either with private property or with socialism. Yet a stationary state, in fact, as well as by definition, would not know any necessary disturbance. Assuming that we are in a stationary society, and want to stay in it, the size of the tool making group will pose no problem—the matter is determined by replacement requirements.[4] In the same way the money flows, as we shall shortly see, need not disturb us. Trouble begins when growth begins. Growth begins, barring technical change, when *net* new investment begins. Net new investment *ceteris paribus* means a tool making group in excess of replacement requirements. Upon these observations we may base our entire analysis. The clue to our present problem lies in two factors—growth and time. The deceptive nature of the stationary state—in terms of which the matter is usually discussed—is due to the fact that growth is excluded while time becomes unimportant. Naturally,

[3] E. F. M. Durbin, *The Problem of Credit Policy* (New York, J. Wiley & Sons, Inc., 1935). D. H. Robertson, "The Monetary Doctrines of Messrs. Foster and Catchings," *Economic Essays and Addresses of Pigou and Robertson* (London, P. S. King & Son, Ltd., 1931). H. T. N. Gaitskell, "Four Money Heretics," in *What Everybody Wants to Know About Money*, ed. G. D. H. Cole (New York, Alfred A. Knopf, Inc., 1933).

[4] The assumption that people "want" to stay in the stationary state, of course, begs the main point.. See the discussion of limits to the use of capital in Chapters III and IV.

if we rule out the sources of trouble, it is easy to conclude that no trouble exists.[5]

The fundamental conclusions of this chapter may be summarized as follows: A flow of money saving, constant in amount, in a society in full employment equilibrium, will *in itself* cause no price disturbance whatever. A constant *percentage* flow, on the other hand, can entail special problems. But in any event, while individual acts of money saving not only need not disturb equilibrium, but are generally essential to it, yet saving, if it is effective, will result in growth and growth entails a price level problem. Assuming that we regard approximate price stabilization as a desirable policy, it is doubtful if there is ever a perfect adjustment. But consequent frictions need not be of serious importance if our society is a *smoothly continuing* one.

The assumption of continuity is, however, crucial and leads on to the main line of our study. For it is obvious that modern industrialisms—of the type, at least, that we have had hitherto—do not expand smoothly. Furthermore, the widest proportional fluctuations are well recognized to occur in the durable goods industries and these industries overlap to a large extent with our "tool making" group. Discontinuity in the production of instrumental goods is found to be a source of much monetary disturbance. We are thus brought back to the consideration of a fundamental problem: What is the ideal size of the tool making group? Why is its activity discontinuous? The reader uninterested in sequence analysis may omit the remaining monetary discussion and pass to Chapter III. Nevertheless it should be borne in mind that though a large part of the monetary disturbances treated in the remainder of the present chapter are causally secondary to discontinuous investment, and though in the present treatment they are only mentioned, they are not merely neutral but on the contrary may prove important aggravations of basic maladjustment.

[5] As an example of maximum confusion in the treatment of these points see J. E. Meade, *An Introduction to Economic Analysis and Policy* (Oxford, The Clarendon Press, 1936), Part I, Chapter I.

(1) Saving, Investment and Income

A tendency to cause unexpected disturbances in the flow of money and in the relation of income to prices has been attributed to: (1) "hoarding"; (2) any act of saving; (3) a change in the amount, or rate, of saving; (4) depreciation charges; (5) profits; (6) bank interest; (7) intermediate transactions, or "B," payments; (8) repayment of bank loans and debts in general; (9) reinvestment of profits. Other costs could be considered but the difficulties raised by them are analogous to those of the nine types mentioned and need not be elaborated. It is clear that all the phenomena listed could occur to a greater or less extent in various kinds of socialism and must therefore pro tanto be considered in the generalized treatment we are attempting. In this section we shall study the contention that any act of money saving must cause price disturbance.

In order to focus attention upon the precise question involved, let us first consider a series of acts of saving-investment which are entirely unproductive—that is whose final product does not enter into the price system at all—say some species of armament. Suppose further that the economy is in full employment equilibrium with a stable population and that initially there is no saving whatever. Capital instruments are supposed either to last forever or else there are no capital instruments. We may further simplify by supposing that all payments are wage payments.

In such a condition let us suppose that consumers are either persuaded to save in order to buy government bonds to pay for armaments; or else that a socialist planning board simply imposes a tax on individuals in order to raise funds for new weapons. The problem in either case has two aspects: Real and monetary. In the first place the workers must be transferred to the new industry. In the second the funds must be forthcoming to pay them.

To make the matter a little more specific let us assume that our society consists of one hundred thousand men, each receiving a dollar per day, and producing in each period consumer's goods worth in the aggregate $100,000.00.[6] Let us then say that they are persuaded or forced to save $20,000 and give it to the state. Consumer's expenditure will obviously be lowered to $80,000 and it would certainly appear that there would be price changes and/or friction of some sort.

Even in this initial case, however, the matter largely hinges upon expectation. Socialist planners may have arranged to cut consumer's goods output by $20,000.00 simultaneously with the imposition of the tax and to transfer a proportionate number of men, previously employed in making consumer's goods, into an arms factory. The drop in expenditure in such a case will merely *follow* the real transfer. There need be no price change and no economic friction.

In a "free exchange" system, results will be a little different. In the case of private investment the first act of saving, or an increase in the amount of saving, may find the economy unprepared. There will then be unexpected losses in the consumer's goods industries. But if the saving is effectively invested, investment goods output will begin to increase. Men released by the depressed consumer's goods makers will be rehired in the investment factories. There is, of course, likely to be considerable friction in the process, but it must be realized that the depression in the consumer's goods industries is not merely unavoidable in most such cases but it may also be a *necessary* part of the real process of transfer.

Let us return, however, to our state arms factory, after the first act of saving. Twenty thousand men, we may suppose, are now working at making arms and they must receive (if wages are unchanged) $20,000.00 at the end of the first "day's" work. This $20,000.00 has been provided by the initial act of saving. Yet when the men have received their first armament pay check a new problem presents itself. Consumer's income will once

---

[6] A much more elaborate and careful version of this model is given in the appendix of this book. It is hoped that it will be consulted in places where the text seems incomplete.

more be $100,000 but the output of consumer's goods is only $80,000. Clearly, if all the consumer's income is now spent on consumption, there will be an inflation of consumer's goods prices and (in a "free-exchange" society) pressure toward re-expansion of the consumer's goods industries.

It is obvious that if price and other disturbances are to be avoided a single act of saving will not suffice to make a *permanent* transfer. As soon as the $100,000 total income ($20,000 armaments plus $80,000 consumption) has been received, at the end of the first day's work, a new campaign must be begun to coax, or force, another $20,000 out of the hands of consumers. This in turn will be paid out in the next period to armament workers and must be offset by yet another act of saving—and so on *ad infinitum*. In such a *continuing flow* of saving-investment each new act of saving not only does not (in itself) cause any disturbance but is in fact *necessary* if disturbance (in this case inflation of consumer's goods prices) is to be avoided.

The writer has found that the majority of purchasing power "lag" theorists—as Foster and Catchings and Major Douglas— usually assume that for every dollar of consumer's income there is somewhere a dollar's worth of consumer's goods being produced. Such an assumption is only appropriate in a society in which there is no net saving.[7] In a continuing society workers in the "tool making" sector receive disposable income but do not produce consumer's goods. Were their spending not matched by someone's saving, there would be immediate trouble. Of course, if we assume that there is somewhere a consumer's good for every consumer's dollar of disposable income, every act of saving would necessarily cause some trouble. But in a continuing system, with a constant amount of saving, such an assumption is incorrect. It is probable that the failure to grasp this important but elusive point lies at the base of two thirds of the mistaken views on the subject.

[7] Strictly speaking, even with no net saving, replacement workers receive consumer's income which must be offset elsewhere by depreciation.

We reach the conclusion that under our rigid equilibrium assumptions the process of saving-investment may be regarded as the continuous turning over of a species of revolving fund. In terms of our model, $20,000 is saved each "day" and paid out in the next day to armament workers who may spend it.[8] But their spending will be offset by the saving of yet another $20,000 and so on. Furthermore, if we leave out price and wage change and continue to think of a strict equilibrium, the size of this revolving fund will *determine the relative size of the "tool making group."* It is the link which connects money outlay with the shape of the industrial structure. To return to the question of whether or not *any* act of saving will cause disturbance, we see that a single act of saving, in an economy which has not hitherto saved, or an increase in the amount of saving, imply (if they are to be effective) a real change in the size of the tool making group and a real disturbance which may or may not (depending on expectations and planning) cause friction. But once we settle down to a flow, constant in amount,[9] then each act in itself does no more than maintain the existing distribution of resources. There is no real or money disturbance.

(2) Transaction Payments in the Stationary State

The conclusion that each act of saving in a constant and continuous money flow causes no difficulty has been reached on very restrictive assumptions. In the first place we have

[8] We must avoid, however, getting the idea that the makers of armaments are the ones who necessarily spend while workers in the rest of the economy do the saving. In fact anybody may be a spender or a saver. It is curious to note that the armament worker who saves may often, in a sense, be employing himself. For if he buys a $500 bond—foregoing that amount of (say) beer, the money may be paid in to the government, and paid back to the very factory in which he works in order to buy guns which he is making. Thus after two transfers his own money comes back into his hands—to be saved or spent again. It is for this reason that I refer to the process as the creation of a revolving fund.

[9] As shown in the appendix a constant percentage flow entails special problems for, if income is rising, the saving of each period (though a constant proportion) will yet be greater in amount than that of the preceding period. See appendix, p. 107.

almost completely abstracted from the problem of transaction payments which has been so prominent in the literature, and in the second place we have side-stepped the problem of growth by supposing that the output of our series of acts of savings-investment did not enter into the pricing system. These omissions must be rectified and we shall first consider the problem of transaction payments in itself (abstracting from growth), just as we considered saving in itself. We may then combine the problem of transactions and the problem of saving, as they occur in a growing world, and see what results.

Following the usual approach we shall begin with Gaitskell's and Durbin's refutation of the crude version of major Douglas's "B" payment theory.[10] We assume that there is full employment equilibrium in a stationary society with no technical change, and we begin with three "stages" of production called—solely for convenience—"spinning," "weaving," and "dyeing." There are no costs of production other than wages, and, at the end of the third stage, the completed product is put on sale. Will there be sufficient monetary purchasing power to meet it?

	"Monday"	"Tuesday"	"Wednesday"	
"Dyeing"			$100	$300, final price
"Weaving"		$100		
"Spinning"	$100			

It is easy to see that in a world in which the processes of production are unchanged and *indefinitely continuing* there will be no trouble. Some have argued that since the completed good comes on the market on "Wednesday" priced at $300 (total money costs incurred) there will not be purchasing power enough to buy it. For on "Wednesday," it is maintained, only the "dyeing" stage has paid out income and that amounted to

10 Cole, p. 280.

but $100. "$100 cannot buy a good priced at $300"—so runs the Douglas A + B theorem in its most incautious expression. But in a continuing system this is definitely not true. All the stages of production are at work simultaneously. As the finished good comes on the market, at the end of the dyeing stage, a new good is being begun in the "spinning" industry, and a half finished one is being worked on in the "weaving" industry. Since all the workers are employed simultaneously their total income in each period can buy total final output. This can be seen by adding the wages paid in each vertical column—each "day."

Economists sometimes stop the demonstration at this point, but to do so omits nearly the whole question. Even before leaving the stationary state there is another difficulty to be dealt with. Many people object to the formulation just given because it omits the existence and effect of certain "residual" costs. Attention is usually focussed upon profits. As a result the applicability of the difficulty to socialist states is frequently overlooked. But there are numerous other costs—as depreciation—whose behavior in this connection is quite like profits and which may be found in monetary societies of all sorts.

Using profits, however, as the easiest example, the argument runs as follows: "Wages are paid out *while* the good is being made and *before* it comes on sale. Therefore wages can be used to buy the good. Profits, on the other hand, are only made by *selling* the good and cannot be distributed till *afterward*. Thus profits are always one lap behind and, unlike wages, do not pay for themselves." This argument is at least as old as T. R. Malthus but, like the formulation of the Douglas theory just discussed, it is clearly invalid in a stationary state.

Let us take the final, or dyeing, stage as an example. We will suppose that the other two stages have labor costs alone, but that in the final stage only $75 is paid out as wages. The remaining $25 will be charged as profit *when* the good is placed on sale. Thus on "Wednesday" only $75 will have been paid out in that stage, yet the final sales price will be "marked up" by $25—giving a total price of $300. It might appear that total purchasing power disbursed on "Wednesday" would be $275, and, since the final price would be $300, this price obviously could not be met. Such a doctrine, however, as J. R. Commons and many others have indicated, is a mistake.[11] In a continuing stationary system, which is already adjusted, "yesterday's" profits help buy "today's" goods. The profits received on "Tuesday" plus the wages of "Wednesday" equal the price of "Wednesday's" output, and so on *ad infinitum*. The addition of profits, depreciation, etc. introduces income streams of a different turnover from those previously existent. But in the stationary state all such differences cancel out. As with Professor Knight's argument regarding the "period of production," the intervals are no longer important since the net effect is a steady flow.

A similar analysis may be applied to every one of the nine sources of difficulty with which we began, excepting only net saving-investment. "Hoarding" will cause no trouble provided each dollar hoarded is matched by one returned. Debt repayment causes no difficulty if matched by an equal flow of new loans. Depreciation charges may coincide with replacement expenditure. Interest is managed like profits. Loops and whirlpools cancel out. And so on.

It must be pointed out, however, that analyses of this sort do not tell us how our society got into equilibrium. In reality, after a disturbed period, replacement may be discontinuous, cumulative tendencies in either direction may exist, and there could be numerous other disturbances. The stationary state is thus in many ways a question-begging device. But it does show that none of the various costs mentioned need always cause trouble, and it is a most convenient springboard from which to analyze the more important case of an expanding society.

[11] J. R. Commons, *Institutional Economics* (New York, The Macmillan Company, 1934), p. 535.

(3) *Expansion*

Let us now move into an expanding state in which there is a flow of productive net new saving-investment. At once a host of difficulties arise. Let us first take profits and return to the diagram given above regarding "spinning," "weaving" and "dyeing." Only now we will not suppose a continuing system but rather that the good completed on "Wednesday" is reaching the market for the first time. How is profit on this good to be earned?

To many theorists the reply is quite clear. The profit will arise because of lower costs due to increased efficiency. "If the new process is not more efficient," they will ask, "why is it being introduced?" Nevertheless a counter argument is frequently made that, if there be no increase in MV, a fall in the price level, due to increased production, will, even with lower costs, exclude a certain margin of possible investments which otherwise might be desirable, and cause a degree of price dislocation and ensuing friction which could be avoided. Most writers of the school we are examining base their analysis upon a simple expanding system without technical change, and without changes in factor combinations. Professor D. H. Robertson concedes that such a procedure is perfectly valid—provided we remember its limitations—and we shall accordingly proceed on that basis for the time being.[12] Profits, then, in the remaining demonstration, will not be assumed to come from lower costs. They can only be earned if, somehow, sufficient monetary purchasing power is distributed *in time*.[13] We will return to changes in price and in factor combinations shortly.

Consider once more the case of the "final" stage on "Wednesday." Only $75 is paid out as wages, and a profit "mark up" of $25.00, ex *ante*, will be made before the good goes on sale. This time, however, as Commons points out, there is no yesterday's

---

[12] Robertson, p. 149, note.
[13] We are not dealing here with value theory and the likelihood that "pure" profits would in any case probably be competed away.

profit to come to the rescue.[14] Unless we have dishoarding (a change in velocity) or the creation of new money (for example bank credit) the sales price normally to be expected cannot be covered. In a continuing stationary flow, income payments overlap, profits do not change, and there is no difficulty. But with an *increment* of new expansion the profit set—*looking forward*—is not necessarily matched by any equivalent *current* outlay.

Before considering methods by which the difficulty can be met, it should be pointed out that profits are by no means the only costs which behave in this way. There are depreciation charges, interest, obsolescence, amortization, etc. etc. With all of these, in the type of world we are considering, the mark-up of the increment runs ahead of purchasing power disbursed *unless* some other force intervenes. The writer cannot understand why it appears so difficult for many economists to grasp the difference between the behavior of costs in an expanding state and their behavior in the circular flow, or after complete adjustment.[15] The difference is exactly that involved in the distinction between the ex *post* equality of "saving" and "investment," and their ex *ante* divergence. In an expanding society prices marked up, *looking forward*, even though set by the best accounting practice, are not necessarily matched by the disbursement of equal current disposable income. That is ex *ante*. But if the price level falls and if everything is once more adjusted, then there is "by definition" an identity. That is ex *post*. Keynes' remark, with which we began this treatment, is "indubitable" ex *post*. It need not be true ex *ante*.

If the difficulty just indicated were universally true, however, the economic system, assuming only a minimum of institutional friction, would probably have been fatally checked long ago,

[14] Commons, p. 535 et seq.
[15] It is suggested that there are two possible reasons: (1) Orthodox Marshallian value theory speaks of price as a resultant—the idea of "pricing," of "setting a price" is foreign to its picture of the entrepreneur; (2) the difficulties we are here discussing are ethically "neutral" whereas the "hoarding" analysis serves as an excellent point of attack against the wealthy and capitalism.

and, leaving aside price change for the moment, there must be some method by which the problem has been met or at least ameliorated. Two principal possibilities exist. The first is pointed out by Professor D. H. Robertson in refuting Foster and Catchings.[16] Foster and Catchings employed a very special case involving an initial rise in prices. Robertson showed that the price rise might induce changes in profit expectations and hence in velocity. In that way profits could be met. Apparently because the overlapping time periods of Robertson's demonstration were considered to violate the rules of the Pollak prize contest, his essay was not given a final mention. But realistically speaking we have here a possible factor of great importance—the repercussions of expectations upon velocity. However, Robertson's first case is a special one and does not, in the writer's opinion, furnish a sufficiently generalized solution to our problem.

The next possible answer is given by Robertson, Durbin, and, most dramatically, by J. R. Commons. Commons points out that we are led quite astray in using circulatory diagrams and blood stream analogies. These give a false idea of the payment sequence. In fact what we have is a "forecast and repetition" system of bank credit with considerable elasticity.[17] In consequence, the entrepreneur, or socialist state trust, is able to borrow in advance the money with which to meet costs.

Common's solution may be applied to a much larger range of cases than mere profits. In particular it meets the problem of "B" payments in an expanding society. Returning to the diagram given above we will see that it is not only the profits of a "final" stage which cause trouble in expansion. The difficulty begins from the start. Perhaps industrial units may be financed from past saving. In that case they will run into no difficulty regarding operating capital. But, as we shall shortly see, such a process would involve considerable repercussions on the rest of

---

[16] Robertson, pp. 53-55; W. T. Foster & Waddill Catchings, *Profits* (Boston and New York, Houghton Mifflin Company, 1925).

[17] J. R. Commons, pp. 546-49. Of course if the banks lack sufficient reserves there will be trouble, but we cannot discuss the paradoxes of a "gold" base here.

the economy.[18] Let us, instead, assume that the units borrow
their working balances. We will find in that case a surprising
amount of credit needed to finance the production of a $300
good.
For example:

"Spinning" borrows $100 to pay labor
"Weaving" borrows $100 to pay labor and $100 to pay "spinning"
"Dyeing"   borrows $100 to pay labor and $200 to pay "weaving"
$300   + $300 = $600 total debt
(Interest, profit, depreciation, etc., and repayment are omitted)

In this example $600 is needed to finance the production
and sale of a $300 good. The actual result would depend on
the payment sequence employed. What we have shown is no
more than the well known fact that the total value of transactions ("B" payments), and balances held to meet them, vastly
exceeds the value of final income and output. But the potential
importance of the repayment problem is immediately apparent.

Leaving aside repayment for the time being, we must return
to one aspect of the profits–interest–depreciation problem.
It is frequently said that such costs are not normally *borrowed
in advance* and therefore, speaking of the whole of society, the
necessary purchasing power to cover them is not forthcoming
soon enough. As long as one concentrates attention upon the
producer's side of the market this objection, *in an expanding
society*, has considerable weight, but Robertson and Durbin
provide the answer. The seller may not borrow such costs in
advance but the *buyer* may—and in that way they can be
covered.[19] Mr. Durbin sums the matter up in a footnote: "It
is curious to notice that if at any moment it were necessary
to increase production from a stationary situation . . . the necessary circulating balances would have to be provided for at every
stage, including that of direct consumption." (italics added)[20]

[18] Robertson, p. 160.
[19] *Ibid.*, pp. 157, 160.
[20] Durbin, p. 37. I have omitted the words "with general unemployment"
because the same difficulty arises in maintaining prices in an *expanding* system
with full employment.

We reach the conclusion that, under the simplified assumptions in which this discussion has so far been carried on, the apparently "obvious" equality of *ex ante* prices with current disposable income is only likely to occur *looking forward*, in an expanding society, if there is a more or less constant expansion of bank credit to consumers as well as to the producers. This conclusion is inferentially conceded by Professor von Hayek,[21] and it should be noticed that it also holds good for a planned socialist state.

(4) Availability and Repayment of Bank Credit

Before relaxing the rigid assumptions regarding costs, factor combinations and technique, under which the conclusions of the preceding section were reached, it is necessary to meet certain objections to our solution taken on its own terms. We have in each case escaped the problem by bringing in bank credit. But it may very well be objected first that the banks may not be willing to lend enough, second, that they may not have the opportunity to lend, and thirdly, "how is the credit ever going to be repaid?"

It is of course clear that if the banks pursue too restrictive a policy, deflation will in any case result. It is also evident that any "inability" of the banks to lend must be understood as inability with reference to sound and eligible borrowers. But bearing these qualifications in mind, it should be understood that we will be dealing here with something a bit more fundamental than mere mistakes, or unduly restrictive bank policy.

The orthodox money and banking text book model of an expanding equilibrium assumes that capital for fixed equipment comes from private long term saving while funds for working capital (and no more) are advanced by the commercial banking

Mr. Durbin's treatment of this whole problem in the first and second chapters of his *Problem of Credit Policy* is much the best single comprehensive discussion of the issues which the writer has encountered anywhere. Professor Robertson's Foster and Catchings' essay is more incisive but less generalized and convenient from an expository point of view.

[21] F. A. Hayek, "The Paradox of Saving," *Economica*, May, 1931.

system. On such assumptions as these it is not difficult to work out models of smooth expansion and samples are given in the appendix. However, everyone knows today that the widest possible divergences may occur both in an inflationary and a deflationary direction. Sometimes they may not lend enough, sometimes they lend too much, and sometimes they may not lend because they have not been "asked" by acceptable borrowers.

Of the cases in which the banks do not lend because they have not been "asked," one of the most important is the reinvestment of profits. It might appear that reinvestment is merely one aspect of the saving problem and, if part of a steady flow, would cause no trouble. Professor Robertson points out, however, that, if the reinvestment is used to cover not merely fixed costs but also working capital, the banks will find it *pro tanto* more difficult to make the necessary loans needed to maintain the price level.[22] This problem arises wherever non-bank investment is used to cover working capital as well as fixed investment. Difficulties would be particularly likely in a full employment economy where the potential margin for extra credit expansion would be much restricted.

A somewhat similar problem can arise in the case of repayment of bank loans. It is well recognized that barring the injection of new money or the exchange of "debts" for stocks, or other "equities," the *totality* of debt can never be repaid in any one period without stopping the entire economic system. Repayment can only be made by a few borrowers at a time, and, if collapse is to be avoided, must be matched—barring changes in M or V—by new bank loans. Yet it is possible to construct models—on very abstract assumptions it is true—in which it will be impossible for the banks to find the necessary commercial outlets. An example is given in the appendix. The solution to this difficulty, in so far as it has a solution, lies in the making of a new loan to the very borrower who has just repaid his loan. Such a conclusion is not as strange as it sounds. Any

[22] Robertson, p. 160.

realistic appraisal will lead to the conviction that, taking the system as a whole, the "continuous" borrower is far more nearly the norm, both practically and theoretically, than most banking texts are quite prepared to admit. The illusion of final repayment comes from two factors—shiftability and seasonal swings.[23]

CONCLUSION

Dangerously abbreviated though the preceding discussion has been, it is likely that some readers have found it too long, and that many points have been blurred by necessary details of explanation. We must therefore stop and summarize. The first thing which will strike the economist is the extreme abstraction of our model. We have assumed no change in taste, technique, or factor combinations, and, save in the case of the "beginning of saving," a marginal propensity to consume of unity. Likewise "hoarding," and changes in velocity, have been treated only incidentally. Obviously such assumptions are far removed from reality and our concluding task must be to relax them, and to evaluate the effects of such a relaxation upon the theory itself. Nevertheless these are the assumptions usually made (though sometimes unconsciously) by writers on the subject, and the author agrees with Professor Robertson that a theory has a right to be considered initially on its own terms. Let us therefore, before making our final modifications, run over the model we have found it necessary to construct.

(1) There is a constant value flow of real and money saving-investment.

(2) An equally constant and equivalent corresponding growth of the population. The rigid and abstract type of expanding economy we have been working with permits no rise (once initial equilibrium is reached) in the standard of living per head.

(3) A steady flow of replacement.

(4) All transactions balances are borrowed in advance from the banks.

(5) Profits, capital charges, etc. are borrowed in advance

[23] Robertson, pp. 157-8.

from the banks by sellers, business purchasers, or consumers. An increased velocity (as suggested by Robertson) may also at times be supposed for dividend and other similar payments.

(6) No loans are repaid; or else if repaid the same sum is reborrowed from the banks in the next period; or else debts are cancelled in favor of "equities."

Looking over this case, and the alternate case of stationary equilibrium, it is immediately apparent what an immense number of other possibilities there must be and how very far from obvious or necessary may be the usually assumed identity of prices ex ante and current disposable income.[24]

But now let us relax our assumption and introduce technical change, changes in taste and changes in factor combinations. These, of course, by the introduction of lower costs make it possible (within the limits of institutional friction which cannot be detailed here) to adapt society to falling prices.

The writer has found, in the course of protracted argument with unorthodox monetary theorists—and with some trained economists as well—a tendency to resent the introduction of the factor of change as being something quite fortuitous dragged in by the heels. This attitude may be attributed to two main factors: First, the process of growth is often visualized as mere extension. Second, the unorthodox writers in particular are apt to be tacitly assuming that no price calculations (or no "reasonable" price calculations) should ever be disappointed. If, for example, a man makes his calculations on the assumption that,

[24] Miss Gertrude Stein has spoken of the "final simplicity of excessive complication." It is curious to note how extremes link up in this discussion. The Social Credit—Foster and Catchings literature is, of course, replete with errors. Yet fundamentally when Major Douglas says that there is an "inherent flaw in the pricing system" he means much the same thing as the orthodox principle that increased production without changes in M V means a falling price level. This is especially clearly seen in Gaitskell's essay (see note, p. 296). Likewise when Douglas refers to the "unliftable first mortgage of the banks upon the productive system" he is implying almost the same thing as the established doctrine that the totality of debt cannot be repaid, at the same time, in any likely circumstances, without causing a collapse. To say this is, of course, not to adopt Douglas's methods of getting a "debt free" economy. In the writer's opinion these would be almost entirely ineffective.

while costs decline, sales prices will not drop, no degree of lower costs will save him from some disappointment regarding profit in the event of price reduction. But it is by no means self-evident either that business men make calculations on this basis or that the degree of "disappointment" need be serious.

In the next chapter we will begin to study the actual relationship between growth and change, and it will be apparent how exceedingly unreal is the idea of growth as mere extension. The real difficulty of the price level problem is that there are no prices "in general." The most usual sequence of events is not symmetrical over-all change but disproportionate expansion in some one line. This necessitates a rearrangement of preference and production patterns and creates disturbances (disappointment of expectation) quite beyond the power of monetary measures alone to remedy.

The present study is not a book on the price level problem. The writer's preference is for a policy of moderate stabilization. It is believed that as a matter of fact the frictions we have been studying, in a continuing system, with any reasonably liberal bank policy, would be of quite minor importance compared with the inherent real frictions of growth itself.

But let us not be too complacent. The possibility of un-expected monetary disturbance is clearly indicated, especially if there is discontinuous development. If the administrators of a socialist state are not prepared to meet the problem—either through ignorance, or because they expect the question to vanish with capitalism, they will find queeer things happening to their social accounting.

It is submitted that the matter calls for empirical investigation, What in fact, for example, has been the effect upon the American banking system of the fact that certain businesses have managed to become debt free? Is there any significant practical importance to the various possible "lags" we have mentioned? Such questions need careful statistical study. It is not enough to work out possible equilibrium models when there are so many other possibilities. It may be concluded that it is very important, in preparing *tableaux économiques*, for example, of the type essayed by Leontieff, not to confine ourselves to the *physical* relationships between goods. A study is also desirable of the actual income periods, actual process of price setting, and actual flows of money into and out of the banks and through the system.

CHAPTER III

GROWTH, CHANGE AND STABILITY—SOME RUDI-
MENTARY NOTES ON THE NON-CYCLICAL
PLANNING PROBLEM

Study of the behavior of money flows in an expanding society has left us with two basic questions: "What is the ideal size of the tool making group?" "Why is tool production discontinuous?" We have found that the fact of discontinuity underlies many other disturbances and it would seem that if only some board of experts could discover and enforce the "right" relationship between tool making and consumption, jerks in the production of instrumental goods would be largely eliminated, and we would have gone a long way toward solving the problem of social stability.

But in the real world we cannot apply the artificial and simplified terminology we have used so far. We must speak not of "tools" and consumer's goods but of capital goods, and consumer's goods. And in searching for the "right" relationship between them, we are confronted at once with the contention that there is no right relation because there are "no limits to the use of capital." This problem will be dealt with specifically in the next chapter. For the present we will merely take it as true that possible limits to the use of capital may be demonstrated as long as one assumes *given* technique and *given* tastes. But the crucial question is: "Can such 'given' assumptions ever be justified?" This question must be answered and in the remainder of this chapter we will lay the foundation for an approach to the problem of a limit by a brief survey of the behavior of consumption and production patterns in an expanding system—i.e., one in which investment is in excess of real replacement.[1] At the same time we will also find ourselves able to mention some of the repercussions of growth and change upon planning.

Expansion, Change and Planning

Everyone is acutely aware today that an economy can be organized on a system of nearly pure rationing. So far as mere mechanical stability is concerned there is little compelling reason why the consumer should be consulted at all. When, therefore, we assume that some effort is being made to conform production to the consumer's tastes, we *pro tanto* limit the generality of our study.

Again it is perfectly possible to think of a society in which there is absolutely no change in the type of instrumental goods in use, although it is virtually inconceivable that proportions and combinations would not be altered upon occasion. Nevertheless, here too, the assumption of change is a limiting factor.

On the other hand practically every alternative social system now being agitated in the Western World does presuppose some technical change and some freedom of choice. It is not therefore unduly restrictive to consider the effects of choice and change upon growth, and the effects of growth upon them. Also, it should be clear that the mere fact of "planning" does not alter the fundamentals of the problem. All we will have done is change the method by which we hope to reach a solution. Still the question would remain: Plan or no plan, how can we foresee the consumer's wants accurately in a growing world?

As a first step in the discussion of this problem it is desirable to run over some of the more or less unconscious psychological assumptions often lying behind our theory of value. At the present time most economic theorists try to take the empirical fact of choice for granted without inquiring into the fundamental reasoning behind it. The "indifference curve" approach

---

[1] Technical change, of course, could make possible net expansion from replacement funds alone.

tries to record preference objectively without asking any of the fundamental "whys." But indifference maps are not prepared or studied solely out of curiosity. Presumably there is some end in mind, and one of such ends is the hope of developing an analysis to help in predicting and planning for changes in the demand pattern. Yet such prediction must imply some sort of stability over time. The question is—what is stable? It cannot be mere relative volume of purchase for that alters with expansion. In spite of ourselves we are bound to be reasoning, albeit unconsciously, or tacitly, in terms of something a little more fundamental.

Stated in the crudest and most unqualified manner I believe that one set of assumptions often underlying a good deal of economic writing on demand runs somewhat as follows. It is assumed, to a greater or less extent, that every man has in his head a "preference universe" in which, ideally, would be tabulated all the possible combinations which he would choose of all possible goods known to him at all possible levels of income given all possible combinations of relative prices. Proceeding on this line any change in the price of any one article, whether due to a change in production functions, or otherwise, would produce a shift in the whole pattern of actual purchases. An indifference map for an individual might be described as a "section" across such a preference universe. In the same way, by aggregating individual preference universes, one produces an aggregate system of preferences for a given society as a whole. It is not maintained that anyone ever explicitly indulged in quite so abstract and mechanical a vision. Nevertheless something of the sort does underlie certain treatments of the problem.

Such a more or less Laplacian concept is also often applied to the theory of production. Each entrepreneur, theoretically, is assumed to know the technical results, under a given state of science, of all possible combinations of all known factors. Give initial price values to these factors, and confront the entrepreneurs with an aggregate preference universe of the type just described, and the whole ponderous calculating machine ticks off the "right" answer. It is along some such lines as these that economists have worked out much of our theory of stationary equilibrium.

Another concept often employed in analysis of this sort has very important repercussions upon the modern social outlook. Frequently—for example in Frank Ramsey's celebrated "Mathematical Theory of Saving"—economists balance the "disutility" of labor against the "utility" of consumption. The corollary frequently drawn is that men spend eight hours a day in purgatory while they "work" and the remaining time in paradise while they "consume." It is an easy inference that it does not much matter what a man has to do on his "job" as long as he does not do much.

When we apply to the problems of social planning the preference/production calculating machine concept, and the "job" outlook toward labor, we soon discover how they operate to minimize and obscure the real magnitude of the task. The stationary state becomes viewed not as an intellectual tool or historical occurrence, but as an actual equilibrial tendency and it is easy to give it a certain ideal value. Consciously or unconsciously, "planning" is looked upon in many quarters as a means of obtaining some certain fixed social pattern or adjustment which need not thereafter be altered. Once the "right" answer is reached, it is supposed, we need trouble our brains no more. As a result the task of the planners (under certain sets of values at least) is unduly simplified, while, in the same way, the "job" concept of labor operates to obscure the universal presence of pressure group problems even in socialist states.

Let us, however, reexamine the preference/production calculating machine. It is tempting to define "unchanged taste" in terms of an unaltered relative preference "universe." Such a universe could be thought of as remaining unchanged, under appropriate conditions, even though the actual market patterns of prices and production were altering. But careful thought will show that even this much of stability is denied us.

Obviously technical change—the intrusion of a new method, or product, into the system—would operate not merely to change market patterns of purchase but also the fundamental "universe" since there would be one more good to be considered. But, as Professor Knight has pointed out, when we start talking of human beings, rather than mathematical assumptions we cannot, even if we exclude technical change, speak of fixed wants—or, as we put it here, a stable preference universe. The difficulty lies in the "*spontaneous*" emergence of new desires.[2]

The writer does not believe that if the process of net new investment is somehow arrested, endless changes in consumption and production patterns would thereafter continue. But suppose that net investment and growth does somehow get under way, even "excluding" "technical change,"—what will happen then?

A satisfactory answer to this question would require a line drawn between growth and change which in fact scarcely exists. Looking at the matter from the production side, a very little reflection will show that there is no sharp distinction between the regrouping of existing factors and what we call "innovation." The extremes, to be sure, are clearly enough demarked. It is easy to distinguish the invention of the atomic bomb from the addition of an extra pair of horses to a cart which must go over a steep hill. But like so many apparently clear distinctions this one will be found to break down at the margin. "Invention" can only be distinguished from a simple changing of factor combinations by the use, as a standard, of some intuitively evaluated degree of novelty.[3] Even if we exclude "invention," simple expansion will entail a constant shift in production methods, since a change in *scale*, in the real world, means a change, at the least, in the proportion in which factors are combined.

[2] Cf., F. H. Knight, "Ethics and the Economic Interpretation," *The Ethics of Competition* (New York, Harper & Brothers, 1935), pp. 31 ff. As will be seen below when we begin to argue in terms of actual market behavior the word spontaneous must be severely qualified. However, in terms of "pure" theory I believe it justified.

[3] Cf., J. A. Schumpeter, *The Theory of Economic Development* (Cambridge, Mass., Harvard University Press, 1934), for a discussion of this problem.

The matter becomes even more complicated on the demand side. With varying elasticities of demand, general increase means a change in relative amounts purchased, and, further, it will be found that as society gets richer old desires are sated and new ones "spontaneously" spring up to take their place. Increasing wealth may give rise to rarefied contemplation, or complicated vice, but whatever form the process takes, new terms will constantly be added to the problem. The human mind cannot be thought of, even abstractly, in the mechanical manner with which we commenced. We need not so much a theory of static relative comparison and tabulation as a theory of *emergent desire*.[4] We can no more speak of unchanged taste in an expanding world than we can "exclude" technical "change."

The conclusion for social planning is not very optimistic. Any growing society which consults the consumer, and does not merely condition him like an automation, is likely to have its plans upset by unexpected changes. So far as prediction goes, we are thrown back upon the statistical study of observed routines of change in hopes that these may turn out to have a certain stability over periods of time.[5] How long, remains to be seen.

We cannot in the scope of the present volume go into the task of working out such a theory of emergent desire. Certain ideas already mentioned, however, can be briefly referred to. On "theoretical" grounds it has long been understood that demand for luxuries during a boom is likely to increase faster than demand for staples. Over time, rarities become luxuries, luxuries necessities, and erstwhile necessities drop out entirely.

In the same way the National Resources Planning Board has

---

[4] This would embrace both "spontaneous" and "induced" change. The distinction between these two terms can only be made in a very rough and approximate way.

[5] The cynic will of course maintain that the whole thing is a matter of propaganda and that nearly all wants could be inverted by a sufficiently strenuous campaign. But if (note the qualification in the text) we do not carry our propaganda to the extent of such drastic conditioning as Huxley's *Brave New World*, it is submitted that even the most expert high pressure campaign can fail.

made a courageous attempt to forecast changes in the pattern of wants on the assumption, among others, that each group will "automatically" assume the taste pattern of the income group into which it is moving as its wealth increases.[6] The use of income—elasticity curves is also fairly common—i.e., quantity purchased is plotted on one axis and national income upon the other, price being assumed unchanged. In our era of "administered" prices such curves are about as relevant as any. But of course we can never leave the basic *ceteris paribus* assumptions, and it must not be forgotten that particular industrial expansions are nearly always carried "on the back" of some new industry, or group of industries—to say nothing of the "spontaneous" changes already mentioned.

Whatever the chances of working out an empirical theory of effective prediction, there is one thing we can be sure of: As the economy expands or contracts, any system consulting the consumer will show great variation over time in market purchase and production patterns. Good "A" which last year absorbed one fifth of the national money income may this year receive but one tenth of it. Both failure to grow and absolute declines are to be expected.

The pattern in a particular year might be as follows:

and in a succeeding year

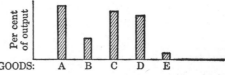

As long, also, as regional specialization exists there will consequently be very considerable differences in relative prosperity

[6] See National Resources Planning Board, *The Structure of the American Economy* (Washington, D. C., 1939).

between regions and the same is obviously true of industries. We do not have simultaneous over-all prosperity or decline. The disturbing results of this fact have two important aspects—mechanical and "cultural."

It must first of all be noticed that if, for reasons yet to be discussed, the various rates of expansion and contraction, for society as a *whole*, do not offset one another, a *net* decline of income and employment will ensue.[7] If this decline is important and prolonged the familiar "incapsulatory" process of secondary deflation will set in. Unless it is offset the whole system may be plunged into a severe depression. Dynamic equilibrium therefore requires that particular industries always rise and fall at offsetting rates. But anyone familiar with the actual data as Burns' *Production Trends* or Fabricant's *Output of Manufacturing Industry*,[8] will know how difficult it has been to find any such symmetrical growth in the real world. Thus a socialism attempting to follow shifting demand patterns would probably have to be on guard against deflation.

The second disturbing aspect of changing demand and production patterns need not be concerned with any *over-all* instability whatever. It is obvious that, provided there is no net change in either direction, an economy which has once adjusted itself to a large volume of "frictional" unemployment need not thereafter suffer industrial fluctuation. But even if there is no frictional unemployment, and no fluctuation, serious cultural disturbance is still possible in a world of expansion and change. It is this disturbance which forms the basis of what we now call the pressure group problem.

There is a naive supposition in the minds of many people that the pressure group problem would not exist under socialism. The writer believes that this extraordinary oversight is largely due to the "job" concept of labor already referred to.

[7] From the standpoint of "pure" theory such a net shortage can only be due to "friction." But see the discussion in Chapter IV.

[8] A. F. Burns, *Production Trends* (New York, National Bureau of Economic Research, 1934). Simon Fabricant, *The Output of Manufacturing Industry* (New York, National Bureau of Economic Research, 1940).

The "job" concept—the balancing of eight hours of purgatory ("disutility") while on the job, against sixteen of paradise ("utility," "consumption") when off of it—is a fundamentally unreal attitude although there are unfortunately certain types of work for which it is appropriate. Protests against the concept range from Carlyle to Professor Knight. It totally overlooks the possibility of creative work, of the joy of building a career, of the satisfaction of achievement. The fortunate man does not have his life divided as supposed. He is the man with interesting work who "plays" as he labors. Not the worst criterion of an ideal society would be one in which the largest number did absorbing work—but to pursue this point would lead us far afield.

As long as one follows the example of many economists and reasons in terms of "utility" versus "disutility," it is easy to conclude that an equalitarian socialism would experience no individual insecurity. If a man simply grinds out a certain amount of uninteresting "work" in order to hurry back to "leisure," it would look as if he would not much care whether he worked in industry A or industry B—all would be equally disutility. It follows, then, that changing patterns, necessitating the abandonment of old lines for new, would cause no trouble.

The error of such a conclusion is easily shown. In the first place simple self interest might still cause trouble even in an ostensibly equalitarian society. For real equality is forever unobtainable. Even though everyone receive the same money wage there may be immense differences in perquisites, if not in perquisites, in title, if not in titles and public honors, in the secret sweets of power. One need only assume that some, or all, of these rewards are roughly proportional to the value of a man's skills to society in order to show sources of possible friction. For if a man derive his power and prestige from his gifts as a designer of locomotives, let us say, he will not look with any friendly eye on the introduction of buses and aircraft which strike at the roots of his eminence.

Even if we leave aside self interest of this sort, there is a man's taste for his profession, his pride in its achievement, and his special skills. His *artistic* sense, as well as his self interest, may be outraged by their abandonment. A changing pattern of preference may leave many an erstwhile important or happy man muttering stranded as a "back number" and robbed of his most precious possession—the pride of, and in, his work. To be sure there are people who approximate a pure administrative type. Distinguished above all by their superior adaptability, they can organize anything for the sheer joy of doing so. They will not object to change but rather to the lack of it. However, most people are not so elastic.

That some individuals will be hurt by the changes which benefit society as a whole is a universal phenomenon of human societies, and it is equally universal that the persons thus adversely affected will try to prevent the changes if they can.[9] Be the matter one of protective tariffs, restrictive planning, "Capitalistic" sabotage, or narrow trade unionism, the security-motive runs through all cultural life like a thread. Prestige, power, creation—these are the things men want rather than mere consumption—"Honorable service" says Bernard Shaw—but what if one's particular line of service be no longer useful? Only by overlooking all such frictions of change can we possibly conclude that institutional arrangement can avoid the conflict of general and social welfare.

Cultural conflicts of the sort just mentioned may only be indicated in the present study, but before completing our chapter, we need to consider one further aspect of taste patterns in an expanding world—the question of over-all lags in consumption. One aspect of the problem is summarized in Lord Keynes' "normal psychological law." As income rises, it is supposed, consumption rises but not as much. This law is today usually qualified by recognizing the fact, indicated by Professor Samuelson, that the "lag" is a short-run affair and that after a shorter

[9] It is true that unemployment benefits, social security etc., mitigate this friction and furnish our chief hope of keeping it in tolerable bounds. But the analysis just given in terms of prestige, career, and the "instinct of workmanship" show, that it will always be potent.

or longer interval the average propensity to consume appears to rise more or less "spontaneously." [10] Our problem here is to outline some of the forces to which this "law" may be due.

If we were to draw a line reflecting the growth of output and the behavior of consumption the results (leaving aside the effects of deflation) are generally supposed to be somewhat as follows:

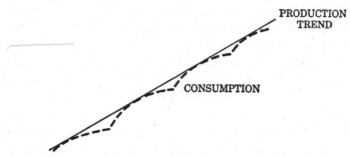

It might appear that such behavior would of necessity be a purely capitalist phenomenon since a socialist society might have less individual reason for saving. However, the unstabilizing factor is not the absolute level of saving but the *rate of change*, and, as long as some individual saving is permitted, its failure to rise *pari passu* with output could cause trouble. To be sure if the volume of saving were very small a failure to rise with output might have negligible effects, but a socialist state with an important volume of saving would probably have to be on guard against a deflation from this source just as it would have to provide against one resulting from shrinkages of income due to changes in taste or technique.

The writer is not convinced that the behavior of consumption levels in expansion can be quite so readily described as is thought today and he submits that there is room for considerably more investigation.[11] However, taking the problem as

[10] P. A. Samuelson, "Full Employment After the War," in *Post-War Economic Problems* ed., S. E. Harris (New York, McGraw-Hill Book Company, Inc., 1943).

[11] For example, Dr. Terborgh in his *Bogey of Economic Maturity* (Chicago, Machinery & Allied Products Institute, 1945), gives consumption ratios for boom years—as 1929—much higher than average.

given, we may ask what would be some of the factors producing such a lag in consumption? We have spoken earlier of the attempt to predict changes in the pattern of demand by the assumption that the individual acquires the tastes of the economic group into which he moves. But such a process takes time. At first when a man has a "raise" there appears a boundless margin. It is only after an interval that new tastes arise to plague him. For some hardy and frugal souls they never arise. But the majority of us *eventually* assume the new pattern and this fact has, in the writer's opinion, very considerable repercussions upon the "scientific" doctrine of the diminishing marginal utility of income. Be that as it may, during the interval of adjustment consumption can lag. Save in a very poor and regimented society of strictly conditioned robots, the writer can see no reason why the same difficulty could not arise under socialism.[12]

A second way of looking at the case is more capitalist in nature. It would assume not that we have a lag in consumption, but that we have defined our consumer's goods and preferences too narrowly. High up, it is submitted, among the satisfactions which a man hopes to attain is the feeling of "security" for himself and his family derived from having a "nest egg" of investments or money. As the individual's income rises, the *relative* marginal utility of other consumer satisfactions declines, while that of hoped-for security rises. Part of an additional increment of income may be spent, say, on a new suit; but after the most intensely felt consumer wants have been satisfied, the individual begins to worry about providing for the future. Since most people feel that the way to attain "security" and provide for one's future is to refrain from consumption, it follows that in the short run, as income rises, proportionately less and less of each increment is consumed. This is an important explanation, it is submitted, of Keynes' "normal psychological law" of consumer's behavior. It is all very well to

---

[12] Of course as stated above in the text the less the proportion of saving the less the significance of the "lag."

assume that demand for satisfactions *in general* is infinite, but to do so does not prove that demand for *particular* satisfactions is infinite. If you ask a man if he wants a case of champagne he may say "yes," but if you ask whether he wants a case of champagne *instead* of an insurance policy, he might very well say "no."

Of course, as Keynes has demonstrated, we may all keep from consuming, but whether our hoped-for "security" will be achieved thereby is another matter. It is also painfully obvious what a frail protection the desired nest egg may be, even if attained. But as long as people *think* they will reach this "security" by not consuming, the propensity to consume could conceivably be kept so low as to prevent the utilization of full productive possibilities. One might carry the matter further and show how, once the desired cash balance or nest egg of investment has been built up—once the consumer deems the future sufficiently provided for (for the time being), and if the short-run maladjustments are overcome, consumption would once more increase. In this way one would show a possible explanation of the statistically observed paradox that the "long-run" marginal propensity to consume is greater than the "short-run" marginal propensity.

CONCLUSION

The main points made in this chapter may be very briefly summarized. We have assumed that it is possible to demonstrate limits to the use of capital as long as one sticks to the severe static assumptions of "given" technology and "given" wants. We have found, however, that in an expanding world there is no sharp theoretical line between "innovation" and changes in factor combinations, and in the same way we cannot speak of a definite fixed preference universe. New desires "spontaneously" intrude themselves as society gets richer. We are thus thrown back upon empirical study of social habits of adaptation in hopes of developing a technique of (short run) prediction.

Applying these principles to the problem of social planning, we found that any state which attempts to consult the consumer can have its plans upset by unexpected changes in preference and production patterns. Changes in the pattern are essential, integral and unavoidable parts of expansion *per se*. Expansion cannot be discussed, even abstractly, without reference to them.

The effects of changing patterns upon social stability, in any system consulting the consumer, were threefold: (1) the possibility of general deflation due to a failure to expand and contract at offsetting rates; (2) severe cultural friction and pressure group problems due to the impact of changes in demand upon individual and regional specialization, and the consequent changes in relative prosperity; (3) deflationary over-all lags in consumption due to the time taken to "get used" to more income, or special tastes which do not require anything beside money to satisfy them. All these disturbances operating together may produce severe upheaval in any expanding society which consults the consumer.

But still the question remains to be answered: Do these modifications, throwing severe doubt as they do upon our theory of spontaneous general equilibrium, make it impossible to speak of *any* "right" relationship between consumer's goods making and other forms of economic activity? The question cannot be further postponed.

CHAPTER IV

A RIGHT PROPORTION?

We now come to one of the most fundamental questions in economics: Is there any limit to the socially desirable rate of real saving? In the preceding chapter we have laid the foundation for a solution by showing the inseparable nature of growth and change, and we also pointed out that we must abandon our previous terminology of "tool makers" and "consumption goods makers." This second point is very important. For it becomes forever impossible to draw a satisfactory and definite theoretical line between capital goods and consumer's goods, or even between investment and consumption. If the end of production be the presentation of desired stimuli to the minds, bodies and souls of the population, where can we draw a sharp distinction between a meat packing plant producing meat to yield "meat satisfactions" and a sculptor producing statues yielding "statue satisfactions"? Furthermore, business cycle research shows that the durability of an object is frequently a far more important consideration for the problem of stability than its place in the structure of production.

Yet though problems such as these have been well recognized and exhaustively treated, economists who have taken the extreme position that there is no distinction between "factors" of production have usually been forced in the end to the conclusion that in the diagnosis of actual situations some rough "commonsense" line must be drawn between "capital" or "investment" goods and "consumer's" goods. The writer submits that one source of difficulty lies in the fact that (as is also the case with "income") different definitions are needed for

44

different purposes. The concepts, for example, which would be satisfactory for a tidy system of social accounting might not be satisfactory in a study of motivation. Even the distinction which at first glance seems clearest—the line between goods bought for personal satisfaction and those bought to yield future pecuniary income—is filled with pitfalls. For practically everything known to man, including labor, or labor power, has under some circumstances been bought as an "investment."

The writer wishes to submit, however, that the analytical difficulty of such problems far exceeds their practical importance. He suggests that we follow the example of the statisticians and draw a rough line following the most usual customary procedure, and that we proceed with our study on the assumption that some more or less arbitrary but reasonably satisfactory distinction can be made. This may appear an unjustified evasion of a major difficulty, but I believe that it will be found that the treatment of the remaining chapters will not suffer unduly therefrom.

(1) Limits to the Absorption of Investment

Assuming then that we may distinguish, in some general manner, between investment and consumption, and between investment goods industries and consumer's goods industries, the question of a "right" proportion and a limit remains to be settled. In terms of the organic analogy with which we began it would seem that the idea that there is no limit would be the equivalent in rationality of maintaining that an otherwise normal man could usefully have an arm twelve miles long. But analogy is not argument and much more needs to be said. Let us first make our terms clear. We shall be discussing not whether there is any abstract timeless limit to the use of the capital stock, but where there is always a boundless demand for any sized flow of current investment—regardless of its relative proportion to the rest of the economy. In other words we wish to determine whether, as a matter of theory, it can be said that it is possible to have, relative to demand, a "real" limit to the useful flow of *current* effective saving. Psychological barriers—as time, or liquidity preference—are recognized as possibly stopping accumulation before the "real" limit is reached, but for the present we abstract from such forces.

Clarity of reasoning requires us to begin our analysis in very abstract and static terms. We assume (1) a fixed labor force; (2) an isolated economy; (3) "no" technical change—as defined in the unsatisfactory "intuitive" manner outlined in the preceding chapter; (4) a fixed scale of wants for society as a whole; (5) no single want has a perfectly and indefinitely elastic demand; (6) the economically significant [1] portions of capital goods are made by the combination of (a) a capital goods making machine, (b) raw materials, and (c) labor; (7) such machines eventually wear out and must be replaced; (8) the capital goods making machine replaces itself but some labor is required to aid it in doing so.

On these assumptions it is possible to sketch an approach toward the demonstration of a real limit to the absorption of investment.[2] One method is as follows. Suppose we begin with a machine making machine X and a scale of wants a, b, c, d . . . n which require the use of capital goods A, B, C, D . . . N, in addition to labor, for their manufacture. Good A will

---

[1] I.e., the exceptions to this assumption and seven and eight are treated as of the second order of smalls. The argument will be recast in more realistic form almost immediately—see text below.

[2] There is a large literature on these points. See for example, F. H. Knight, "Interest," *Encyclopaedia of the Social Sciences* (New York, The Macmillan Company, 1930-35), Vol. VIII; "The Quantity of Capital and the Rate of Interest," Parts I and II, *Journal of Political Economy*, August and October, 1936; "Diminishing Returns from Investment," *Journal of Political Economy*, March, 1944. On the other side see Oskar Lange, "Interest in the Theory of Production," *Review of Economic Studies*, June 1936; P. A. Samuelson, "Dynamics, Statics, and the Stationary State," *Review of Economic Statistics*, February, 1943. See also F. H. Knight, "Note on Dr. Lange's Interest Theory," *Review of Economic Studies*, June, 1937, and Dr. Lange's reply in the same issue. This latter is the best short summary—in static terms—with which the writer is familiar. I have given an earlier version of my own views in "Professor Knight on Limits to the Use of Capital," *Quarterly Journal of Economics*, May, 1944. Comparison of that article with the present text will show that while I have not materially changed my conclusions, my analysis has been considerably altered and has now more in common with Professor Knight.

be multiplied until an output of "a" is reached at which "b" begins to be preferred to an unchanged rate of addition of A. Thereafter the total "free" labor force is reduced by the number of laborers needed to: (1) maintain and operate X; (2) replace A; (3) operate A.[3] Next B is pushed to the margin where c appears, then C to d and so on. The maximum limit becomes an eventual problem in approximation in which the labor force is divided in the most efficient manner relative both to the scale of wants and technological efficiency, so as to produce a maximum flow of utility.

Reasoning of this sort is open to a multitude of objections [4]

[3] As a matter of expository convenience I have used a form of statement in which the output stream satisfying (relatively) want "a" is first produced in full before work is begun on "b." In fact of course the difference in "rank" may be slight so that while work on A and "a" is begun first, work on B and "b" will be commenced long before "a" has reached the margin where further absolute expansion will be stopped.

[4] A most serious difficulty lies in the fact that there are always pre-existing implements of some sort. See also the exceptions discussed in note 5. Further in the real world both wants and techniques change. These objections will be discussed shortly in the text. At this point, however, we may mention a different set of objections which are concerned with the paradoxes of a zero rate of interest.

If we rule out time and liquidity preference, then a condition of full invest-ment implies a rate of zero. But it should be noticed that a zero rate is not a necessary accompaniment of the idea of a limit. Psychological factors could be supposed to halt accumulation short of the maximum, with or without full employment.

Considering, however, the paradoxes of a zero rate we find the following assertions:

(a) A boundless demand for consumption loans. Zero interest is said to entail boundless consumption demand, therefore to have a zero rate without inflation all goods would have to be "free."

This argument overlooks the problem of repayment. It is true that if men were perfectly indifferent as to who borrowed their money one could always borrow from A to repay B. But lenders do consider the solvency and character of the borrower.

Professor Knight writes in "Diminishing Returns from Investment" (p. 26). "Of course a borrower would have to keep assets adequate to secure the loan, or perpetrate fraud." But surely the supply of such assets is not "boundless" and a very brief reflection will show that if he were going to consume any of the loans he could never borrow enough assets.

(b) Difficulty of valuing permanent income streams. Without interest, it is said, the value would be infinite. Professor Samuelson disputes this conclusion in certain cases of fact, but supposing it to be correct, Professor Schumpeter's answer is simply that there would be "no market" for such things. See my article cited above, note 2.

but serves as a useful point of departure. Prolonged reflection, however, has convinced the writer that it is useless to continue the analysis on such terms. The basic reason is the inseparable nature of expansion and change already spoken of in Chapter III.

We may recast our argument in more realistic terms as follows: Instead of assuming a *given* scale of wants we assume the following course of events: Increasing the supply of capital good A increases the flow of consumption utility "a." Thereupon the relative marginal utility of "b" will rise and B will be made. Increases in "b" will next cause a demand for C to produce "c." So far we have followed our previous example. But now the production of "b" and "c" together may lead consumers to drop "a" entirely. Yet as "a" is dropped, a new want "e" might appear while B began to decline and "f" appears, so on *ad infinitum*. At the same time in which these "spontaneous" demand changes are occurring, factor combinations are also being changed so that a perpetual process of reorganization would seem to take place even if there be no change in population and no "invention." It is easy to conclude that, leaving aside the difficulties regarding effective demand detailed in Chapter III, the process of constant reorganization thus outlined could absorb an indefinite flow of net new investment.

The above account isolates, in the writer's opinion, the valid essential core of the contention that there is no limit to the absorption of investment. Various subordinate arguments are detailed in the notes but are submitted to be of secondary

---

Professor Knight argues that a zero interest must exclude the possibility of creating any further permanent capacity at a "less than infinite cost." I submit that this involves a confusion of "permanence" with "capacity." The fact that a "tool" is permanent does not mean that it yields any value return. The accumulation of a sufficient stock of permanent appliances, even at a less than finite cost, could conceivably make them free goods. Compare Lange's reply to Knight, noted above.

I assume as self-evident, vide Schumpeter, Böhm-Bawerk, Keynes, that nonpermanent goods would yield no *net* return but would not be "free" since their production costs would have to be net. (One can, if one wishes, include time or liquidity preference as a "cost" and thus argue that a zero rate is impossible. But the argument would then be one of conflicting assertions—it would not prove that a zero rate was *per se* absurd.)

importance.[5] Leaving these secondary points to one side it is submitted that the entire basic argument is founded upon a tacit *ad hoc* assumption whose truth is by no means self evident. It must be assumed that no matter how large the proportionate

[5] There are certain assumptions which, if correct, would negative the idea of a right proportion, or a limit based on technological factors, aside from the dynamic argument of the text. Thus it may be maintained that the flow of "capital" goods or "investment" goods would be of such a nature that its products would yield never vanishing increments of final output. The series might be thought to approximate some finite limit or alternatively an infinite value might be ascribed. In the first case, however, Mr. Ramsey's calculations of a limit become relevant. See Frank Ramsey, "A Mathematical Theory of Saving," *Economic Journal*, December, 1928. But in the second case, apparently, any proportion of saving would help raise the standard of living, albeit very slowly. Since the mathematician is always free to "assume" what he wishes, the writer can only say that he does not believe in the practical likelihood of such a flow—especially if "innovation" be excluded. Furthermore even if we grant the possibility of the concept it still does not avoid the necessity of *some* limit short of zero consumption. For if everyone always saved *all* their income, everyone would starve to death.

Again, it may be said that capital goods cannot be used in the "period" when they are made, but only in the next period. Thus, if we disregard all expectation, any amount of current investment needed to absorb current planned saving can be made today, because the losses will only show up tomorrow. This, of course, is formally correct, but proves nothing in practice. The Biblical injunction to take no thought for the morrow is seldom obeyed so literally that investment is turned out without regard either to past losses or future prospects.

Certain other more reasonable hypothetical cases must also be mentioned before reaching the core of the argument. The first of these is a condition of indefinite waste. Analysis along such lines, as Veblen pointed out, explains why war is so admirable a solution to the problem of capital "glut." Whenever we assume an insatiable demand for some one satisfaction *relative to all* others, and assume that its supply can be "indefinitely" increased by the use of more capital, then we get a case in which an indefinite amount of capital can be used. However, except in short periods of religious or patriotic frenzy, the writer cannot conceive of such a condition. If demand were truly "insatiable" for any one type of satisfaction, would not that satisfaction be the only thing consumed?

A more plausible case may be constructed by assuming not "insatiable" demand, but perfectly elastic demand for some one satisfaction or several of them relative to all others, and combining it with a broad definition of capital. We may define capital as "desirable things of any sort," or in other terms equally comprehensive. The Venus de Medici, the Ford plant, the Hope diamond, and a hamburger stand will all be equally capital goods. This enables us to by-pass to some extent the problem of dividing the labor force. We can, then, think of a condition in which the demand for a stock, say of objets d'art, is "unlimited," but the demand for current additions to the stock is limited—the reason being that the current enjoyment of other satisfactions is preferred to a higher *rate* of addition (investment) to the total stock of art objects. If increased planned saving, in this case of perfectly elastic demand, should be accompanied by a sufficient increase in the rate of purchase of objets d'art (i.e., a sufficient raising of the demand line), then any amount of savings-

flow of net new investment, the rate of change of tastes and production patterns will always and inevitably be fast enough to absorb this investment. In other words the doctrine requires us to assume that a high saving society is not merely per se a high wanting society, but a changeably wanting one. Mere existence of a given scale of intensely felt wants is not enough.

It must be admitted that the analysis of Chapter III does give some support to this idea and warrants the assumption that wants and production patterns "spontaneously" alter to some extent as income rises. But Chapter III does not support ad hoc assumptions as to the rate of change. We must moreover distinguish between the case in which consumer's outlay—however small in absolute terms—is rising and the case in which consumer's outlay is suddenly reduced. A constant rise, as we have seen, will bring about some "spontaneous" change. But to say that any flow of investment can always be absorbed implies that even if consumer's outlay were suddenly decreased the rate of change of taste and obsolescence would necessarily be fast enough to absorb resulting investment. Thus a rise in effective saving-investment from 20% to 98% of total national income, in the absence of "dynamic" factors, and of the minor exceptions mentioned in the notes, would have to be accompanied by a rate of change of taste simply staggering in rapidity. But the writer sees no mechanism inevitably linking increased ex ante saving with more rapid change in taste. Professor Knight argues that if time enough be allowed for planning, the matter can be handled. His statement may be defended with some plausibility in reference to a single monumental increment of investment. But the very way it is put suggests the possibility of a rate of addition too rapid to be planned for successfully.

The fundamental conflict traces back, it is submitted, to the assumptions one selects regarding the behavior of the consumer

investment might be absorbed. Unfortunately, such an automatic coincidence of increased planned saving with an increased demand for some particular satisfaction requiring additional capital cannot always be presumed. Further, the writer finds it difficult to conceive of a demand curve which would really be perfectly elastic throughout its entire length.

and of the market. If we look at the matter in terms of a fric-tionless preference/production calculating machine such as was described in Chapter III then saving-investment absorbing a more or less indefinitely large fraction of total income might appear possible—*provided* that consumer's outlay is rising in absolute terms, and that the process starts at or above a sub-sistence minimum. But this slot machine view of the economic process is not very realistic. A true theory of emergent desire has to be cast in very different terms and would certainly call for a tremendously slower rate of change and of saving. The *rate* of change of taste and production patterns is an institu-tional, cultural, almost political variable.

Those who conclude that the rate of change of wants must coincide with the flow of investment, however large, are apt to be reasoning in terms of the mere uncoordinated idle desires and whims of an individual rather than his usual market be-havior. Such arguments imply the situation of some oriental despot in an immensely wealthy empire or Aladdin confronted with his lamp. On this basis it is easy to conclude that any amount of investment can be absorbed. Leisure (for the despot) is no objection for "leisure" can be a great waster—look at Versailles or Capri. Ascetic contemplation is no answer for even a Yogi burdened by wealth could forsake Samadhi long enough to say "Let my fortune be used to relieve as many and as worthy wants as possible." There would be no trouble in disposing of it then. Reasoning about the individual in a vacuum overlooks the problem of how a man's effective wants are in fact changed and how they are fitted into the market.

Shah Jehan could pour the wealth of all India into the Taj Mahal and a similar process would easily absorb any flow of investment, always remembering, of course, that the population must consume enough to remain alive. But the ordinary indi-vidual, buying in the ordinary market, is not so situated. He must wait until the tiny pull of his changing demand is co-ordinated with that of thousands of others, and in this regard we must remember that in the economic "election," which we call the market, voter-buyers have the referendum and the recall but not the initiative. New desires are not developed by the public so often as they are intruded upon them. Men are more generally "sold" on a new line, than they are found increasing "spontaneously" the demand for an old one.

From all that has been said it can, in a sense, be stated that technical or real limits to the absorption of current investment are a matter of cultural "friction." This may be particularly well seen if we refer to the matter of "hoarding." In a primitive society the net result of a rate of *ex ante* saving in excess of the amount of investment currently absorbable would be temporary or permanent waste. In a capitalistic world, however, such an excess of "planned saving"—if it did not destroy the banking system—would result in an accumulation of purchasing power in somebody's hands, and it might be said that if people were not willing to allow funds to accumulate, the pattern of wants would be bound to change sufficiently. Formally this is correct in a frictionless world. But the accumulation of funds we are speaking of here cannot—save "by definition"—be jammed into such categories as "avarice" or "liquidity preference." Money in the case we are discussing accumulates *passively* simply because, in the short run, consumers or producers have lacked the imagination or the energy to develop effective new wants with required rapidity.

We may thus conclude that the "real" limits to the absorption of current investment are not fixed and eternal. There is, formally speaking, no single state of full investment even if we omit "innovation." The economy may be thought of as passing through periods in which, for the time being, we can approximate a "given" preference system and in such conditions the demonstration of a static general limit becomes *pro tanto* temporarily relevant. But the matter is not mechanical but biological. Unless the cultural frictions are too severe the economy will break out of the deadlock and begin to develop once more.[6]

[6] Due to the factor of inertia in the real world, the emergence from a near-equilibrium is apt to be initiated by "innovation" or replacement boom, but

Mr. Ramsey's "Bliss"—even leaving aside "innovation"—has not one, but many, possible values.

We must be careful, however, as to just how much we dismiss as "friction," and what conclusions of policy we draw from it. "Friction" can include almost anything—for example the fact that we live in a particular space-time system and cannot all be at the same place at once. What is needed is a distinction—never very precise—between friction and *removable* friction. While price flexibility, better knowledge, better organization of the market could conceivably make possible the absorption of a larger flow of current investment, the writer does not believe that any market economy within the realm of possibility could ever be so smoothly organized as to be capable of absorbing any rate of saving-investment which could be thrown into it. It follows that in the world in which we live we can positively assume the existence of technical limits to the absorption of current investment, even though the line in any particular case cannot be precisely drawn.

Such limits are, however, short-run affairs. The "propensity to consume" seems to rise automatically. It is in this connection that the doctrine regarding the "boundlessness" of human wants becomes important. There has been in the past twenty years a deal of loose talk about "ending the economic problem" through the productivity of the machine. But the thoughtful economist must conclude that the economic problem does not need a machine to solve it nor can the machine by itself ever do the job. The problem can be "solved" at any time by the combination of an adequate system of birth control with a good ascetic or epicurean philosophy—i. e., one restraining desire. And in the long run the problem cannot be solved by anything else.[7] To sum up, Professor Knight at times appears to visualize current

the accumulated changes in wants and consumption habits which have waited for expression serve to give an extra "kick" to the upswing.

[7] I mean of course not mere stationary equilibrium but a "solution" in which everybody has everything that he wants.

In this connection the economist should never forget the maxim "tremendous but trite" that we could perhaps make everybody twice as rich but we could not make everybody twice as rich as everybody else.

investment "outlets" as a sieve through which any amount of water can be poured. Many of the Keynesian school would seem to treat them as a glass—holding so much and no more. The writer would regard them as a rubber bucket whose elasticity is not fixed and which *over time* appears to be indefinitely expansible.

(2) A Right Proportion

From the foregoing discussion two very important conclusions emerge: First the absorption of current investment is limited by the current rate of expansion, plus invention, plus replacement, plus obsolescence—all acting and reacting upon one another. The net effects of all these determine the amount of saving-investment currently absorbable. Next this amount is constantly changing. It follows that spontaneous stability in a growing world requires somewhere a mechanism which would ensure that current *ex ante* saving varied, automatically, with changes in the current limit to real investment. Such a mechanism some at least of the earlier writers thought they had found.[8]

Everybody agrees, and we have seen in this study, that in full-employment equilibrium the labor and other resources of society may be thought of as being distributed between two groups: makers of investment goods and makers of consumer's goods. Everyone further agrees that under such circumstances the proportion which one group bears to the other is roughly determined by the consumption habits of the economy—in Keynes's system measured by the "propensity to consume."

To the English classical writers the rate of interest was, of course, set by the supply and demand for loanable funds but on analysis this will be found to have been usually only the most superficial aspect of their theory. Fundamentally these monetary transactions were symbols expressing: (1) the supply of the commodity real saving—a flow of resources currently set free for investment uses by the failure of society to consume its en-

---

[8] The analysis which follows is adapted from my article, "The Future of Keynesian Economics," *American Economic Review*, June, 1945.

tire output; (2) the demand for this commodity fixed by current investment opportunities—in the last analysis the current net marginal value product to be derived from the use of newly produced investment goods. The money rate on loanable funds merely expresses the "real" rate—the excess, figured in some ideal numeraire, of real purchasing power returned to the lender, by the borrower, over that which the lender had originally parted with in making the loan. Monetary changes might distort this "real" relationship but, when equilibrium was once more reattained, the real rate would be reestablished, and money could once more be ignored.

While one cannot be too dogmatic in this matter it is submitted that prior to Keynes probably the larger number of American and English economists believed that the current demand for loanable funds (essentially for the most part demand for the real resources they represented), varied over time with changes in invention, expansion, growth, etc. While John Stuart Mill's view of developed industrial countries as habitually on the "verge" of the stationary state might have been considered extreme, most economists in this country—with varying degrees of optimism regarding the investment outlook at particular periods—nevertheless felt that outlets varied over time, and that a naturally stationary state was at least a theoretical possibility. But if investment outlets varied, how could full employment be maintained?

The answer, it is submitted, would probably have been along the following lines. Current saving behaved like "any other" commodity. When new inventions, etc., temporarily raised the marginal productivity of capital and made it desirable, for the time being, to divert a larger proportion of resources from consumption to investment, the demand for loanable funds (under the assumed conditions thought to be little more than the symbol of the demand for free resources, released by current saving), was raised, and as a result the rate (both real and money) of interest went up. With an increased "price" paid for current saving the amount of current saving "naturally" would increase.

Men would be shifted from making consumption goods to making investment goods and all would be well.

If this process should be reversed, when the new opportunities were substantially exploited, and if no new ones had appeared, a greater proportion of consumption would be desirable. This too would automatically be provided for. As investment opportunity declined the rate of interest would decline. Consumption would rise as investment fell and surplus laborers in the investment industries would be moved back into making consumer's goods. Also reducing the rate of interest might help investment outlets.

Full employment, then, barring "frictions" of adjustment, and the business cycle, would always be maintained by means of a supposed functional relationship between profits, interest, and current savings. If the economy reached a stationary state consumption would rise and the rate would: (1) fall to zero, with no net savings-investment, as maintained by Schumpeter, Irving Fisher and some of the English writers; (2) following some Austrian and Swedish writers, consumption would rise so high, due to time preference, that a certain minimum rate would be maintained since below it there would be capital consumption; (3) other writers, as J. B. Clark, spoke of a "minimum" without giving any very explicit analysis as to what that minimum was or why it would arise.[9] But in any event there would no longer be any net savings-investment and there would be full employment.

There is no need to stress in detail what modern theory and statistics have done to this analysis. It is well recognized today that short-run planned saving does not vary to any appreciable extent with changes in the rate of interest, that the rate of interest is determined by many factors in addition to the marginal efficiency of capital, and does not necessarily move with it; and finally that the marginal efficiency of capital itself is no mere reflection of technical marginal productivity, plus real

[9] This classification excludes writers like Professor Knight who deny the possibility of spontaneous stationary equilibrium.

obsolescence, but a weird hodgepodge of speculative and psychological factors. We may in consequence dismiss the possibility of a spontaneous adjustment of savings habits to change in investment outlet. In an "uncontrolled" market economy, therefore, the positions of "semi-glut" referred to in the previous section are thus seen to be far more likely to be periods of unemployment than periods of stationary social calm. The effects of control will be discussed in Chapter VI. Two points, however, remain to be treated before moving on to cycle theory per se. They are (1) hoarding and (2) wage or price reduction.

Taking the admission already made that limits to the absorption of investment (other than time preference, etc.) are matters of cultural friction, certain writers have deduced that wage and/or price reduction, or measures to stop "hoarding," would cure the difficulty. They do not rely upon changes in consumption habits but stress instead the maintenance of investment by measures to maintain velocity, or else by appropriate price policy.

The writer believes that the weakness here is the confusion already pointed out between "friction" in a purely formal sense and "friction" in the sense of actual obstacles to investment, or to spending, which can really be removed. The "hoarding" of money, of which we have been talking in our model, is as already indicated, a passive result not an active cause—though of course, once a crash begins, it is reinforced by real panic hoarding; and it is hard to predict just what the results of velocity stimulation—as stamped money—would be in the real world.

One thing, however, is certain. The maintenance of MV is not the same thing as the maintenance of either output or "full" employment. The imposition of a hoarding tax could result merely in high prices, a stock market boom, a special demand for land, or various other distortions. It is difficult to visualize the panic of 1929 in terms of a hoarding tax so drastic as to prevent the accumulation of funds. It should however be clear, the writer believes, that such a tax could not per se prevent market collapses and once the collapse had started, inability to accumulate money might well result merely in a high price for other security media. Perhaps this might result in some increase in employment but not necessarily so. The "classical" economists may have been wrong in saying flatly, "Demand for commodities is not demand for labor" but they would certainly have been correct in saying "demand for commodities is not *necessarily the same thing* as demand for labor."

Because of these theoretical inadequacies, plus the well nigh hopeless practical obstacles to a program of forced velocity maintenance, more orthodox economists have preferred to coax money back into circulation rather than force it.[10] For this they have relied upon price and wage reduction. Here, too, there is an elaborate literature which will not be recapitulated.[11] The writer believes that it is quite possible for wage or price reductions to function as supposed, if we have just the proper conditions and payment sequences. But such measures *need* not be successful. Furthermore, if we assume, as one intensely relevant friction, the desire to maintain the present system, then price and wage reductions become dubious tools indeed. What degree of price and wage reduction would have been needed to cure the 1929 crash in any tolerable period of time? Could it have been enforced without causing a revolution?

Those who rely upon price and wage reduction, as practical cures for any threatened depression, are misled, the writer believes, by a confusion of possible dishoarding with the marginal efficiency of capital. While price reduction may cause some individuals to buy *existing* assets at "bargain" prices, it cannot be relied upon to start the production of *new* assets and hence of increased employment. Only *by definition*, it is submitted, in the sense of "zero" or "negative" wages, can we rely upon wage or price reduction so to maintain the inducement to

---

[10] Cf., my *Creation of Purchasing Power* (Cambridge, Mass., Harvard University Press, 1942), Chapter VI, "Velocity Stimulation."

[11] *Ibid.*, Chapter III, "Redistributions and Purchasing Power," § 3, "The Level of Money Wages."

invest as to have a steady demand for capital goods and full employment.

We conclude then that there are moving limits to the amount of current investment which can be absorbed in a growing world but that there is no spontaneous mechanism which would adjust and readjust savings habits to such variations. We also conclude that the various purely monetary methods of maintaining velocity, or the inducement to invest, cannot always be relied upon. It follows that a market economy is not self-adjusting even on theoretical grounds. We have thus reached a point at which we can begin to examine the capitalist maladjustments of the business cycle itself, and when we have completed that task we will try to determine whether comprehensive "controls" would enable the "planners" to do a better job.

CHAPTER V

THE BUSINESS CYCLE—CAPITALIST CASE

Before going further we should summarize the ground we have covered so far in our analysis of disturbance without ever mentioning the business cycle at all. Save in the last section of the preceding chapter we have kept our analysis as broadly applicable as possible. We have dealt with societies which were growing, which consulted the consumer, and which used money. Beyond that no further restrictions were laid down. Yet even on this broad basis, and without reference to special capitalist difficulties, we have seen how growth inevitably entails the possibility of maladjustment.

Our analysis has been in terms of overlapping rates of change. We have seen that in a growing economic organism the stability and health of the whole require that the rise and decline of the component parts proceed at complementary rates. In the matter of money any likely monetary society will probably find it desirable that expansion of total output be accompanied by some appropriate rate of increase in purchasing power—though what this rate may be is a difficult problem. Regarding consumption, it is imperative that the general "level" fluctuate in a manner complementary to "investment" if spontaneous stability is to be achieved. Finally, regarding the changes of taste and production patterns which are an integral part of expansion in a society consulting the consumer, it is obvious that these must in the aggregate, occur at offsetting rates or deflationary pressure will begin.[1]

Yet in the short run the total effects of changes in taste,

---

[1] Inflationary pressure is also possible.

growth, innovation, and production patterns do not necessarily produce a smooth aggregate—nor is the consequent short run demand for "durable" and/or "investment" goods either smooth or "insatiable." This result also holds true of the *spontaneous* individual market demands in a socialist state, but for the present we defer the problem of planned control. Yet, in any event, since the rate of change of consumption does not spontaneously fluctuate sufficiently to offset movements in the demand for capital it follows that we may say on a *priori* grounds that any growing market economy will not be self-adjusting.

In the capitalist world the results of these unstabilizing forces are two-fold. First investment "outlets" may come to be such, relative to consumption, that "permanent" or prolonged unemployment will ensue. This might be described as a slow drying up of the vital forces of the organism and is usually referred to as "secular stagnation." It will be discussed in Chapter VII. Next *average* consumption habits may be such as to give "full" or "more" than "full" employment at the peak of each boom, but, for some reason, each rapid expansion, and disproportionate growth of the instrumental goods industries is brought to a halt. Since there is no adequate spontaneous mechanism which would ensure an equivalent rise in consumption, unemployment and deflation (barring intervention of some sort) must then begin. Our task, in the present chapter, is to analyze the forces which could initiate such disturbances in a capitalist economy.

From what has been said it follows that a depression could commence almost anywhere, and for a number of reasons. All that is needed, for example, is that one major industry be declining faster than others are rising. But in the capitalist business cycle, as such, we do not find merely a series of heterogeneous scattered disturbances. First of all there appears to be a rough uniformity of timing which induces some writers to speak of "waves." Next one finds a still more marked uniformity in the location of major disturbance. It seems pretty clear that in a *major* boom and slump (leaving aside minor inventory cycles) the most unstable part of the economy is the durable goods industries. Speaking broadly we might say that a major boom is a time in which plant, housing and machinery are being installed and a major slump is a time in which they are not.

The apparent uniformity of timing in the cycle seems to the writer an unsolved problem. There are various theories which could conceivably explain the phenomenon—if we make appropriate assumptions. For example there are sun spots, "replacement" waves, the period of "gestation" of capital,[2] and Professor Pigou's reaction time theory. But conclusive evidence is lacking to test the validity of the hypotheses and until we know much more than we do now the question must be left open. The superior fluctuation of the durable goods industries, however, is not so inexplicable and to it we will devote the remainder of this chapter.

In older business cycle literature it has been customary to speak of "capital goods" and "consumer goods" industries, but in view of the growing importance of durable "consumer's" goods, such terminology is increasingly unsatisfactory. Yet even to speak of durable goods industries is likely to give a false emphasis. The mere fact that the durable goods industries are the most unstable does not mean that they cause the instability. We shall, therefore, usually speak here of "expanding industries" and their suppliers and the "remainder of the economy." Such phraseology may not be as elegant as "consumer's goods" and "capital goods" but it is a great deal more accurate. The consumption-investment-interest rate analysis is a fair first approximation but it cannot be pushed too far.

The writer believes that in beginning an "explanation" of the business cycle certain fundamental principles should be recognized. First of all a complete theory of the cycle must be capable of describing not simply any cycle taken at random but the "first" cycle. It is easy to show how a boom grows out of a

[2] The writer accepts Professor Knight's criticisms of the "period of production" as a matter of theory in a *continuing* system. But should it not be obvious that in a system which is constantly being started and stopped, the period of gestation (not the same thing as Böhm-Bawerk's period) may become of great importance?

slump and vice versa. But to leave the matter at that is circular reasoning. Again the writer believes that all exclusive theories of the cycle are wrong. He assumes (though admitting that facts may some day be found to controvert this opinion) that the cycle can be due to a number of varied forces, some of which will predominate in one cycle and some in another. So far as pure theory is concerned, there are at least a dozen perfectly self-contained and (logically speaking) entirely adequate theories of the cycle. The question is which as a matter of fact is most relevant practically. Here is where the statistician and the historian come in. In the present chapter we shall merely summarize some of the major explanations—indicating the manner in which we believe them to be connected in realtiy.

Empirically speaking the problem of the business cycle may be described as expansion *at a faster rate than can be maintained* and, always remembering that the initial impetus may come virtually anywhere, we have seen that most of such expansion (in terms of percentage at least) is likely to be in the durable goods industries. Beginning, then, the task of explaining an initial expansion from full employment equilibrium,[3] it is not surprising to find the first explanation a monetary one. Banking, speculative and price distortions are to this day the most immediately striking features of the crash and one does not wonder that the earlier economists should so often have begun with money. Furthermore, given appropriate assumptions, the purely monetary theory can explain all the observed phenomena.

(1) "Monetary" and Allied Theories

In order to have expansion at a faster rate than can be maintained it is usually necessary to have elasticity in the labor supply and productive system generally. This can, however, be ensured by monetary means alone. Let us begin with a state of full employment equilibrium.[4] Let us next suppose that for

---

[3] This equilibrium may either be stationary—but with a flow of replacement investment—or else "dynamic"—vide my *Creation of Purchasing Power* (Cambridge, Mass., Harvard University Press, 1942).

[4] As to the nature of the equilibrium see note 3 above.

some reason, the banks lower the rate of interest and certain industries begin to receive a large number of loans. These expanding industries, as already stated, may be of almost any type but the expansion will virtually inevitably create a disproportionate derived demand (if no other) for durable goods. Reasons for the disproportion will be discussed in Chapter VI.

As long as the expanding industries and their suppliers receive a sufficiency of credit, they can expand by stealing factors of production from the remainder of the economy. Inflation will of course almost inevitably result but this need not disturb the growing industries as long as they can obtain ever larger supplies of credit at a *faster* rate than the general rise of prices and wages. In that way "slack" can be kept available for further expansion.

The downturn may be given several alternative though not necessarily conflicting explanations. First the banks may run out of reserves—and/or raise interest rates, for example, Mr. Hawtrey's cash lag theory. But conceptually this could be remedied by relaxing reserve requirements to allow indefinite inflation. More difficult to deal with—though still theoretically surmountable by indefinite inflation—is the problem of *excessive* purchasing power. On the supply side, labor scarcity or bottlenecks may put labor groups in such a strong bargaining position that wages will rise faster than prices. In this manner expected profits and the incentive for borrowing are cut off. Next there may be a general rise in the demand for the products of the remainder of the economy—most usually consumer's goods. Because of this increase the remainder of the economy will begin to outbid the expanding lines for productive factors and expansion in those lines and, usually, in their suppliers, will be checked.[5]

At this point it is necessary to make a vital assumption. It must be assumed that despite the fact that the populace is

---

[5] The supplying industries might conceivably find a market in other fields. Especially in the case of the durable investment goods industries their output may be fairly non-specific.

clamoring for the products of the rest of the economy, and despite the fact that there is no shortage of general demand, it will be harder to shift men out of the expanding line and its suppliers, or at least, in the latter case, to transfer the direction of their efforts, than it was to get them into it. If we do not make this assumption, and if we assume, as many monetary theorists do, that at the beginning of a crisis there is both adequate (or excessive) monetary demand and a sufficient (or excessive) propensity to consume, then we ought to expect merely a *shift* of factors, not a slump. There would be waste but not unemployment.

(2) "Real" Theories

The writer is willing to concede that the purely monetary account just given expresses a possible sequence of events. Two weaknesses, however, would seem evident—the beginning and the ending. Why should the banks suddenly lower interest rates and increase loans out of a blue sky? Mr. Hawtrey's explanation is conceptually adequate but circular. In the same way Professor Hayek apparently puts the entire blame upon price level maintenance and a consequent unduly low interest rate. But is the business cycle really only the result of recurrent banking folly?

Again there is the question of the upper crisis. Would indefinite inflation really serve to keep the boom going?

For all these reasons it seems desirable to examine an alternative account of the cycle cast largely in "real" terms. Let us first assume that some new product or technique is introduced into an otherwise equilibrium situation. The product is so desirable, or the technique so cost saving, that high prospective profits are created and the inducement to invest in that line is greatly increased. It might be argued that if the rate of interest be raised the incipient expansion could be cut off. Undoubtedly *some* rate of interest could cut off any expansion. But it should be remembered that a raising of the general rate, sufficient to restrain excessive expansion in the new line, could well cut off desirable expansion in other lines and even conceivably cause unemployment.[6] Let us, however, for the moment merely assume that the interest rate is neither raised nor lowered.

With an unchanged interest rate and high prospective profits in some one line some inflation is almost inevitable. But again, simply to focus attention on nonmonetary disturbance, let us assume no change in MV and in the amount of saving. However, the new line and its suppliers may still expand rapidly and disproportionately. Money for the expansion can come from savings which would otherwise have gone into other lines. A "slack" of manpower needed for disproportionate expansion may be drawn from two sources. First labor displaced in other industries by the shift in demand might be available. Next, if a new technique is involved, technological unemployment could create the necessary amount of "free" labor. For example the introduction of textile machinery in England simultaneously raised prospective profits, and impoverished numerous domestic workers who crowded into the cities. All the requirements for a disproportionate expansion were thus called into existence at one and the same time.

We must next try to explain the downturn of the "real" cycle. It should be clear that the explanations previously given for the downturn of the purely monetary cycle could be invoked here too. Shortage of bank credit, lag of prices behind wages and costs, excessive demand for the products of the remainder of the economy—all could operate. However, it is more usual to concentrate on other explanations. These are: (1) a "lag" in the demand for the products of the expanding line, or in demand "generally" (2) simple relative saturation of the particular investment "opportunity" involved. In Spietoff's phrase "the bucket is full."

While it is difficult to visualize a boom which in fact is unaccompanied by monetary disturbance still an adequate

----

[6] Such a state of affairs implies discontinuous demand, i.e., there is a gap between the effective demand for the expanding line and next most acutely felt want.

model can be constructed. Suppose a new product or technique which deflects to it nearly the whole flow of net current investment. Suppose next that the *relative* demand for this satisfaction is temporarily satisfied, and it ceases to expand, but that the demand for the products of the remainder of the economy and their suppliers does not rise *fast* enough to fill the gap? We could then, theoretically, get deflation without having had any previous inflation at all. The model is extreme but it is a useful check upon excessive emphasis on consumption or money.

There is another fact implied which may prove to be of great importance. The model assumes a discontinuous market demand functions. That is to say new desires, effective in the market, do not automatically appear fast enough to maintain spontaneous full employment. The writer offers as one hypothesis, the suggestion that at the beginning of a boom we are likely to find a number of acutely felt *capital-requiring* wants, but that, as the boom proceeds, the newer wants progressively exploited do not require capital in the same quantity. The result can well be a decline in investment demand despite the fact that "consumption" is constantly increasing.

Whether the suggestion given be accepted or not, there is, in any case, a certain superficial resemblance between the basic assumption needed to explain the downturn of the purely monetary cycle and that of the "non-monetary" versions of the "real" cycle. In both cases we must, in a sense, assume that it is harder to get men out of the expanding line and its suppliers (or to transfer the direction of the supplier's energy) than it was to get them in to it.

But speaking practically—rather than by definition—the resemblance is very superficial. The purely monetary theory implies an inability to transfer men and resources even though consumers and others are clamoring for the products of the remainder of the economy. In many versions of the real cycle on the other hand it is only by definition that we can speak of unsatisfied wants for in the "real" cycle people may not be trying to purchase at a faster rate. In other words we must remember the distinction insisted upon in earlier chapters of this book between mere unsatisfied "wants"—in a vague general sense—and the actual market pattern. Speaking by definition, in a frictionless world, we might say that, if some people were not willing to allow funds to pile up, there could be no downturn. But this sort of talk—true enough in its own sphere—is, as we saw in Chapter IV, largely irrelevant to practical policy. Nor can the difficulty in our model be subsumed, save by definition, under the head of "hoarding" in the sense of avarice or liquidity preference.[7]

One final point remains to be mentioned regarding the "real" cycle. Would indefinite inflation always prevent a slump? Again by definition the idea might be true. For a gigantic disbursal of funds, if it were large enough, and sufficiently reckless of price distortions, could serve to create sufficient demand. However, if we allow for institutional friction, or if we recur to the theory already given and suppose a spontaneous drop in the demand for capital due to the fact that the newer desires effective in the market do not require proportionately as much capital as previously, then very considerable inflation might not serve to bring on full employment, and very considerable increases in V (and P) due say to taxes on hoarding could be equally ineffective.

Returning now to the general problem of the cycle it will be immediately apparent that in describing actual behavior the two approaches which we have detailed cannot be sharply separated. Using innovation, changes in taste, or replacement boom, as the initiator of the expansion, it is clear that monetary inflation and deflation, with all that it implies, can come in to heighten the expansion and accelerate the decline in any cycle. In the same way a rapid upsurge in optimism, and relapse into pessimism serves to aggravate fluctuation. Finally only the force of our current fashionable emphasis blinds us to the fact that depression *could* conceivably be caused by too much, rather than too little, purchasing power. If we assume that it is easier

[7] I mean liquidity preference in a meaningful sense and not "by definition."

to get men into an expanding line than it is to get them out of it, and if we assume that the expanding industry or, more likely, its suppliers collapse faster than others rise, we have the seeds for a depression.

(3) The Basic Problem of Distortion

But we have yet to explain, other than by inference, the reason for the basic distortion of the cycle: *Disproportionate expansion of the durable goods industries.* Why is it disproportionate and what is the connection with durability?

Probably the most fashionable explanations at the present time are that the matter is due to planlessness, or to cumulative mistakes by entrepreneurs, or to consumption lags due to "hoarding"—any one of a group of explanations, in fact, which can in some way shift the burden on to the capitalist institutional organization.

From such a point of view the writer wishes to dissent vigorously. Socialist writers who adopt it are doing their cause no service and may be paving the way for an eventual discrediting of large parts of their practical program. The fact of the matter is that there is something considerably more fundamental than planlessness or capitalism at stake.

In seeking for an ultimate explanation we must introduce a third methodological criterion in addition to the two with which we began. We must recognize that while a complete theory of the cycle must be able to explain the first cycle, nevertheless the problem of cyclical stability—as we find it today after many cycles—is not the same thing as the first cycle. The problem of the first cycle was a largely negative one of restraining overexpansion. The problem of any actual modern cycle is twofold: First to obtain full employment, next, to prevent "over" expansion. This leads us to one of the most complicated and difficult problems in the whole of economics, namely, what is the socially desirable rate of general expansion? [8] We may discuss this best in terms of the socialist business cycle.

[8] Cf., D. H. Robertson, "The Snake and the Worm," *Essays in Monetary Theory* (London, P. S. King & Sons, Ltd., 1940), pp. 109-111.

CHAPTER VI

THE BUSINESS CYCLE—"PLANNED" CASE

During the earlier part of this study we set out to find the "ideal" size of the investment goods industries, relative to consumption, and it was suggested that a planning board able to enforce the "right" relationship could avoid jerks in production to go a long way toward solving the problem of social stability. However the argument of Chapter IV led to the conclusion that there was no a *priori* long run ideal relationship, but merely a series of fluctuating and rather indefinite short run limits. Furthermore we have found that there is no adequate spontaneous mechanism by which short run consumption can adjust itself in an unplanned market economy. But now the question arises: "Can the planners do any better?"

The problem confronting us may be approached from two sides. The planners may (a) try to induce a series of changes in consumption, or (b) endeavor to "smooth out" capital demand. Policy (b), in turn, is capable of yet further subdivision. Investment may conceivably be planned *in advance* so as to produce a smooth aggregate, or else a program of "filling in" or compensatory finance may be adopted designed merely to keep fluctuation within bounds.

The writer does not feel very optimistic concerning the chances of "planning" rapid shifts in consumption. One must remember that short run stability requires not high saving, or low saving, but *variable* saving. The Russian government has shown what can be done toward compelling a high average proportion of saving in an impoverished society. Contrariwise, in the alleged "economy of abundance" of the West, it is certainly arguable that socialism by making life more secure, reducing the motive to accumulate, etc., etc., would obtain a higher *average* propensity to consume. But as far as the cycle is concerned it is frequently not the average but the marginal propensity which is of first importance. Planning may change the average volume of saving but can it change the rate of change? Again, when rapid changes in consumption levels are needed, may the government simply proclaim, "Everyone will now spend money this month" and later announce, "Everyone will now start saving"? Should the government try to do so, could the planners be sure of estimating the results correctly in a free society?

Since most comprehensively planned economies which we have known so far have been very poor in consumer's goods, any slight extra margin allowed the consumer has been speedily taken up. But it remains to be seen whether in a wealthy free socialism you can both lead the consumer to water and make him drink.[1] The more likely choice of a planned economy, it would seem, will be to endeavor to smooth out, or fill in, investment goods demand.

In this connection we are confronted by the choice between planning nearly the whole field of investment *ex ante* to produce a smooth flow—as apparently advocated by Lord Beveridge for example, and the much more modest concept of planning which seeks merely to organize social desires in slump so as to prevent violent fluctuation. In much of the radical literature of today the latter policy is viewed as an unworthy compromise. A deal of ridicule is heaped upon "public works" or "deficit finance," as a crutch which barely enables us to hobble despite the mistakes of the capitalist market. But is this attitude justified?

[1] We are not here discussing the problem of the secular choice between goods and leisure, but of short run fluctuation in consumption levels complementary to fluctuations in investment demand. Of course the workers in the investment industry might be allowed to loaf and draw their salaries during slack times but this would scarcely be good for the morale of the remainder of the economy.

As pointed out in the previous chapter, men usually assume that the "over" expansion of the durable goods industries is the result of lack of forethought. Thus Lord Beveridge has suggested that the instability of the construction trades is due to "many headed control of industry." [2] M. Ilin, in New Russia's Primer, gives a dramatic exposition of how the capitalist order periodically "overbuilds" itself because of "lack of plan." [3] Mr. Kalecki puts the blame upon a decisions lag.[4] Mr. J. A. Hobson blames it on overbuilding due to too much "saving," [5] and so on. Whatever the reasoning the problem is viewed as the outgrowth of the present economic order.

Now it cannot be denied that "planlessness," mistakes, cumulative over-estimate of profits, etc., can cause depression. But is this the whole story? What is frequently forgotten is the possibility of cyclical waste, distortion and/or unemployment in a comprehensively planned state abstracting from the problem of error in forecasting.

To sift the matter thoroughly let us assume that the planners wish to follow not a compensatory policy, but one of anticipatory smoothing out. To further this aim they are willing to license and plan the growth of all industry. Their endeavor will be first to select, or ascertain, the average proportion of saving in their economy, and then so to direct the flow of new investment as to ensure a perfectly smooth flow of demand—and yet give the consumer what he wants. Can the job be done? The answer depends upon the social values to be followed and the circumstances under which the task is undertaken.

[2] Lord Beveridge, Full Employment in a Free Society (London, G. Allen & Unwin, 1945), p. 308. Lord Beveridge in the passage referred to assumes that the "supply of houses does not follow the demand closely." The writer submits that Lord Beveridge in this statement may be confusing need with effective monetary demand.

[3] M. Ilin, New Russia's Primer, The Story of the Five Year Plan, translated by G. S. Counts (Boston and New York, Houghton Mifflin Company, 1931), Chapter II, "Two Countries."

[4] M. Kalecki, Essays in the Theory of Industrial Fluctuation (New York, Farrar & Rinehart, Inc., 1939).

[5] J. A. Hobson, The Economics of Unemployment (London, Macmillan & Company, Ltd., 1931).

In the preceding chapter it was intimated that the problem of stabilizing the business cycle in a society which has already experienced several booms is quite different from that of preventing the development of the cycle in a society still in full employment equilibrium. This point may turn out to be of great importance to socialist states. For the odds are enormously in favor of the prediction that socialist governments, or other type governments advocating the comprehensive planning of society will take office in periods of unemployment, or slack production. Either the planners take over a backward country or else one whose industrial structure has experienced the cycle. In any case there will be slack and in any case they will be faced with the problem of deciding on the optimum rate of expansion.

In order to bring out clearly the essential difficulty let us suppose a very strong case. Suppose the United States governed by a politically omnipotent, and economically omniscient, planning board possessed of every moral virtue. Assume that there is initially no failure of consumption to keep pace with the actual output of consumer's goods,[6] no monopolies or pressure groups, no price rigidities, no inflation, and to give a perfectly clear field no problem of foreign investment or foreign trade. But suppose further that such an economy be confronted with the problem which we now face after the war; a large, newly released labor force, considerable deferred demand, a large potential rise in the output of consumer's and capital goods. This case closely resembles, save in degree, the situation in the beginning of an ordinary boom. Does not the way seem open for peaceful and rapid expansion? Unfortunately one further question remains: How *fast* shall consumer's demand be satisfied?

(1) *The Single Industry*

We may best begin our study of the equilibrium rate of expansion by concentrating upon a single commodity—say hous-

[6] I.e., if *total* output and income drop, consumption may be supposed to drop with it, but while income is rising consumption will be supposed to keep pace with actual consumer's goods output.

ing. Let us suppose that the only houses in existence are palm leaf huts which fall to pieces after a single night and which must be rewoven each day by primitive savages who use only their bare hands in the process. If this were the case there would be no problem of stabilizing the housing "industry" nor of selecting an optimum rate of expansion. The optimum rate would simply be to build as many houses as were needed each day as fast as possible—having due regard to the conflicting uses to which labor can be put. It follows that if our primitive tribe be assumed stationary in numbers, skill, age distribution, tastes, and resources, there would be a perfectly definite daily optimum rate of house production at which the industry would be permanently stabilized.

But now let us suppose that while the tribe still desires a certain number of houses relative to other satisfactions, say 100, that these houses are durable—lasting say ten years. We may also say that house construction is placed under the control of a planning board desiring to stabilize the "industry." Yet we further suppose that the board starts from scratch—that is to say that initially there is not a house in existence.[7] At what rate will the board permit expansion? Putting the matter so baldly of course exaggerates the problem but it is well to get essentials clear and qualifications will soon be added.

A very brief calculation will show that if the board places perfectly smooth housing demand above all other virtues it cannot allow the construction of more than ten houses per period. For each house lasts ten years. If all were built at once there would be no further housing demand whatever for ten years. The industry would be highly unstable. On the other hand, if we build at the rate of ten a year there will be a perfectly smooth demand for an indefinite period. Replacement will take over when expansion leaves off. We may conclude that, considering a single industry alone, the rate of expansion

[7] The problem would not be greatly different if there were some houses already built, but the Board were deciding how rapidly it should make a large addition to the total stock.

consistent with stability is a rate *no faster than the equilibrium replacement rate in full employment equilibrium.*

For example, if in full employment equilibrium, the total relative demand for commodity A would be 500 units lasting 15 years the equilibrium rate of expansion would be 33⅓ units per period. If 400 units for 20 years it would be 20 per period. The calculation may be adjusted to fit not merely given amounts but also given amounts plus given rates of expansion in a dynamic equilibrium. In any event the reason why non-durable industries are more stable than durable ones is immediately apparent. In the non-durable industry the equilibrium replacement rate *equals* the total equilibrium flow. There cannot be either replacement "waves" or a "drop" to replacement requirements. But with durable goods all sorts of distortions and "gluts" are possible.

All this, one may say, is very well. We have "found" the "equilibrium" rate of expansion. But let us look a moment at the other side of the picture. Suppose that there are enough men and resources "free" to build not ten but one hundred houses a year and that the demand for the equilibrium figure of one hundred houses is intensely felt. In that case there arises a fundamental conflict between speed in the satisfaction of consumer's wants on the one hand, and stability on the other. For if the equilibrium rate is equal to the replacement rate, so also *the time taken to attain full equilibrium satisfaction is equal to the length of life of the individual equipment unit.*

The so-called equilibrium rate of expansion will have the following parodoxical results. If we consider the single housing industry alone, a rate of ten a year will leave *"permanently"* unemployed [8] men and resources sufficient to build ninety houses, and it will keep consumers in the streets *for ten years*

[8] The word "permanently" is put in quotes because, if the housing industry were stabilized, as indicated, the surplus portion could, in fact, be diverted to some other employment—were sufficient demand forthcoming. But see the treatment of the system as a whole given below.

Professor Haberler has shown that similar difficulties can occur regarding rapid accumulation of an inventory of "single use" goods.

waiting for shelter. The price of stability becomes "permanent" unemployment and an unnecessary ten-year delay in satisfying the consumer. Yet this conclusion has nothing to do either with planning or not planning. Given slack in the productive system, intensely felt desire for certain durable goods, and a wish to give the consumer what he wants when he wants it, and Lord Beveridge himself with the aid of all H. M. Army, Navy and Marines could not stabilize the construction industry.[9]

(2) The System as a Whole

It is obvious that the dilemma we have given must be subject to a great deal of qualification, but before we commence to make the necessary adjustment let us first consider the case of the system as a whole under equally severe assumptions.

A fundamental cleavage centers about the concept of planning. Is it to be viewed as the means of obtaining some fixed, unchanging "optimum," or "ideal" stationary equilibrium, or is it to be merely an attempt to "rationalize" or "control" a process of eternal change. Are we to shoot the inventors, distribute resources on the basis of "given" technique and taste, and go fishing; or are the planners to toil painfully after the inventors, seeking merely to cushion the shock of their revolutionary innovations and keep social disturbance within bounds? The choice is vital and the writer submits that the delusive air of mathematical certainty which hovers about much planning literature—for example, Mr. A. P. Lerner's *Economics of Control*, and many of the works of Mr. Stuart Chase, derives from a partial or subconscious visualization of planning in terms of the static ideal rather than the eternal process. But even if we think in terms of the static ideal, there could be trouble.

Let us suppose that by the extrapolation of "given" tastes and techniques the planners compute exactly what the demand and production pattern would be in full employment under their

[9] We are at this point excluding public works. I think this legitimate in the initial exposition, for Lord Beveridge seems to imply that "single headed" control of the housing industry could stabilize it—without public works. In view of the model just given I doubt this very much.

ideal of wealth distribution. Suppose that they are absolutely correct in their forecast but that they have taken control in a period of unemployment and/or productive slack.[10] Would they be able to reach the ideal output and distribution, avoid rationing the consumer, obtain full employment, maintain stability, and prevent waste *all* in the same process? The writer does not believe these standards could be met *simultaneously* by any power, even if the planner had full and accurate foreknowledge of the pattern of wants at every stage, and complete control of the processes of production![11]

Let us suppose that the pattern of production and taste in static "ideal" equilibrium, would be as shown in Figure II. Demand is distributed evenly among four consumers' commodities—A, B, C, D. Tools used in the making of these commodities are made by two industries P & Q, and their tools are made by industry X which also replaces its own equipment. Admitting the abstraction of the example, let us ask how we could build up to such an equilibrium without "waste," instability, or rationing.

In trying to give realistic meaning to such a diagram one immediately encounters Professor Frank Knight's very cogent and practical objection that always there are pre-existing implements. In the real world the planners would probably have to do as the Russians did in the Five Year Plan, and begin by using what equipment was at hand to construct industry "X"— the basic tool making industry. But before they went any further they would be likely to encounter the problem of "over" building "X"—for the reasons given with our housing example.

Various other possibilities must be considered. For example, the planners might borrow capital instruments from abroad and shift the burden of possible "over" expansion on to some other

[10] The "productive slack" could come from new inventions previously held off the market.

[11] Professor D. H. Robertson has anticipated portions of my analysis in this connection, "The Snake and the Worm," *Essays in Monetary Theory* (London, P. S. King & Son, Ltd., 1940), pp. 109-111. I do not, however, assume any necessary "forced saving" or inflation in the process I am describing and I believe that the essentials of my model are somewhat different from his.

FIGURE II

	Industry X ("self replacing")	
replacement (10%) or .4 a year	.41	
machines	4	
men	4	
output	4.1	44.1

	Industry P		Industry Q	
replacement (10%) or 2 a year	2	22	2	22
	20		20	
	20		20	
	20	40	20	40

	Industry A		Industry B		Industry C		Industry D	
replacement (10%) or 10 a year	10	20	10	20	10	20	10	20
machines	100		100		100		100	
men	100		100		100		100	
output	100		100		100		100	

Note: Italicized figures indicate current machine demand at a growth rate of consumer's goods output of 20 in A, B, C, and D.

Replacement is 10 each year for A, B, C, and D.

Figures italicized would be different if there were, as yet, no retirement of equipment.

Complications due to inventory accumulation are omitted.

Replacement in X is 4.1 rather than 4 since X is "self replacing."

country. But in order to get our foundation work done, and assuring the reader that more realistic formulation will be forthcoming, let us abstract from these and similar problems. It should be clear that once industries P, Q and X are built—leaving aside the problem of how—the maximum rate of expansion of consumer's goods output for A, B, C, D consistent with final stability is ten a year. But, as before, this entails ten years of rationing and "unemployment." [12]

[12] The reader may be puzzled because in this model unemployment lasts only ten years while in the housing model it was "permanent." The difference lies

It is also noteworthy, in understanding the violent fluctuations of the steel and allied industries which are such a problem in social stability today, to observe what would happen if, at a time of productive slack, but shortage of consumer's goods plant, the growth rate of consumer's goods output and consumer's goods plant, in our model became 20 a year. The steel industry bears a certain very rough resemblance to our industry X. Yet a *doubling* of the expansion rate of consumer's goods, in our model, produces an increase in the demand for X's products of nearly *eleven hundred* per cent—i.e., from 41 to 44.1 [13] units of output.

Obviously different relationships may be assumed for different "stages" of industry and for each supposed relationship one would obtain different values regarding the ultimate magnification of derived demand. But the writer submits that the results given in our model are suggestive, and that the empirical value for magnification likely to be found when the derived demand of hundreds of industries converges simultaneously upon the "higher" stages, in real life, is likely to be exceedingly great. Yet again the difficulty cannot be exorcised by mere planning *if* the people are in a hurry for increased output and if the planners want to give them what they want *when* they want it. Once more the price of perfect stability becomes prolonged "unemployment" and rationing.[14] Is it likely that any genuinely democratic socialism would carry through such a program? Would the program be worth while? Before discussing these issues let us reformulate our dilemma in more realistic terms.

---

in the fact that in our present model the unemployed are gradually absorbed into operating the newly completed consumer's goods equipment as it is completed. In the housing model very little "operating" labor is needed by the completed houses.

We are here leaving aside public works.

[13] A similar problem would emerge if, instead of an increase in the growth rate of the consumer's goods industries, technical change caused a sudden doubling of machine demand on the "first" stage. See my "A Neglected Approach to the Acceleration Principle," *Review of Economic Statistics*, XXIII, May, 1941.

[14] Leaving aside public works.

(3) Objections and Modifications

We may first consider some objections to our model on its own terms—i.e., in terms of an eventual static equilibrium.

It may first be said that one consumer's goods industry could be expanded at a time. But this would still imply rationing. People, we are assuming, do not *first* want houses, and then cars, and then hot water heaters, etc. They might take the goods in that series if they had to, but what they really want, and would try to buy, if permitted, is some of *each* all at once.[15] Furthermore, as we have set up the problem, there is no reason, save the fear of ultimate contraction in the durable goods industries, why they cannot have some of *all* the desired durable goods at the same time—and fairly promptly too.

But it may be urged that we should go ahead and "over" build the durable goods industries, simply discarding excess capacity when it is no longer needed. But is this not "waste"? At least is it not the kind of thing which capitalism does sometimes do now, and for which it is bitterly attacked by left wing economists? Furthermore there are complications from possible replacement waves which cannot be entirely overlooked. That is to say that while the discarded equipment may not be needed for a number of years some day we might have to curtail our standard of living while we stop to re-erect it.[16]

In this connection it should be understood that in speaking of a sudden huge increase in the demand for the upper stages of tool making we do not need to suppose that new plants of that size will always have to be constructed. If socialism inherits a capital goods plant already overbuilt, rapid expansion need not always require the erection of a new plant to meet the sudden convergence of equipment demand. Nevertheless this "peak" load would be a temporary one and though some plants are

[15] In the model of Chapter IV for expository convenience we assumed such a satisfaction in descending order. But in fact the difference in preference may well not be sufficiently great to justify such a procedure.

[16] Vice versa there might be a sudden drop in the aggregate demand for durable goods due to discontinuity in replacement.

already overbuilt to meet it, the permitting of such a "wave" of durable goods demand would not be consistent with planning for perfect stability.[17]

A final static suggestion would be to operate all instrumental goods plants at half capacity all the time and accumulate a stock of capital goods in advance to meet peak loads. The "excess" factors of production in the instrument trades might then be slowly absorbed into consumer's goods making—taking care that they themselves are not used so quickly as to create a further distortion.

To this idea there are two objections. First, if one permits technical change the accumulated stock of instruments might be obsolete before it is needed. Second, even in static terms a series showing the spontaneous demand for capital after many booms had occurred might not be reducible to a regular sine curve but rather to an extremely irregular one whose sinuosities it might be almost impossible to iron out if rationing be excluded.

An entirely different and more "capitalistic" set of considerations turns on the problem of price. It may be objected that, after all, quantity purchased is relative to price and that if the durable goods are priced high enough people will "want" something else. This argument must be taken in two senses. First, it may mean that the planners can discourage demand for durable goods by deliberately pushing up the price to an artificially high level. As a consequence people are led to "prefer" non-durable shelters to the permanent homes they wanted. The second version of the argument would have it that the problem

---

[17] The problem concerns the durability and need for replacement of the equipment inherited. If none of it is in immediate need of replacement, or obsolete, non-durable consumer's goods output could be increased very rapidly to its former peak figure without increasing machine demand at all. We leave aside complications regarding inventory accumulations but it must not be forgotten that it also can "accelerate."

It must be remembered, however, that full employment in the consumer's good industries would not give full employment for the whole of society under the conditions assumed. And a rapid increase beyond the previous maximum would be likely to give rise to further "bunching" of capital goods demand.

is due to an insufficient allowance for future risk in a normal pricing system—i.e., if the housing industry amortized its equipment and charged a high enough risk-profit (pax the income tax collector) during a boom, prices would "automatically" be high enough to discourage buyers sufficiently to slow down purchases to an equilibrium rate of expansion.

In evaluating these arguments it must again be stressed that all the physical means are present, in the case we are supposing, to satisfy the existing demand for durable goods in a comparatively short period, and, further, that these demands have an A priority in the consumers' minds. They are intensely desired in preference to increases in the demand for non-durables, or else the non-durables produced are intensely desired and so there is an intense *derived* demand for durables. Under these circumstances one can of course concede that the planning board by placing an inordinately high price upon durable goods can slow down demand to the "equilibrium" rate. But we began by excluding rationing and, obviously, artificial price manipulation of this sort is nothing more than rationing in another guise.

On the other hand it might be that the amortization quotas, etc., charged by a fluctuating durable goods industry, in order to show a net reasonable average return, would be so high as to slow down demand to an equilibrium rate.[18] The writer believes, however, that, speaking of capitalism, if only the solvency of the owning interest is considered this would not be the case. Perhaps if there were some way in which the full social cost of spasmodic unemployment could be embodied in the market price of unstable durable commodities it might help to smooth out demand and lead the consumer to live in a tent rather than a house. Possibly the task might be accomplished by the levying of tremendous social security taxes on unstable industries during a boom. But let us not forget the social consequences of the

---

[18] It is for reasons similar to these that the present American income tax system may be said to discriminate against the fluctuating durable goods industries.

equilibrium rate even if such a price policy could give it to us.[19]

Would it not be better to let the boom go ahead (provided it did not turn into violent inflation) and fill in the "gaps" thereafter with public works of some sort? But can this not be done in capitalism? [20]

Before we consider such problems we must discuss briefly some objections to our argument in terms of the eternal process. Such arguments turn on the "boundlessness" of human wants and have already been examined in earlier chapters.

It might be argued, for example, that when one set of desires has been satisfied another will take its place. Granted that rapid satisfaction of the demand for equipment to produce good A has "over" expanded the capacity of the tool making industries, why does not the demand for good B now take over? True we satisfied the demand for "A" "too fast" and "over" built the supplying industry. But can't "B" be satisfied equally "too" fast, and then "C" and so on. Since, also the supplying industry is likely to be fairly non-specific, there seems no reason why it could not be switched from supplying one line to supplying another. Complications from overlapping replacements are obvious, but not a sudden drop.

The basic assumption behind this argument is that there exists a smooth and continuous series of effectively organized market demands producing a smooth aggregate. Furthermore, if we wish to argue in terms of "boundless" demand for capital, or absorption of investment, we must assume a smooth, constant shift in the demand pattern, furnishing always the necessary obsolescence.[21] As has been earlier pointed out, the writer does not believe that either of these assumptions is empirically true as a general rule.

The final complication comes from "innovation." Assuming

[19] I.e., possible prolonged unemployment (barring public works) and an unnecessary denial of consumers.

[20] The difference, if any, between the response of the two systems in this connection seems to me chiefly ideological.

[21] Barring the special cases mentioned in Chapter IV.

a "new" technique or product, in the sense of a really major departure from accepted method or satisfaction, we are likely to find a discontinuous demand function in its most aggravated form. What new private personal desires, for example, could have been rapidly made effective in 1930 to take the place of the capital requirements of the automobile and allied industries after the relative demand for them was temporarily filled?

(4) Conclusion

In this chapter we have set out to find whether a comprehensively planned economy could do a better job of relating consumption to investment than a capitalist order. We saw that the spontaneous demand for investment varied greatly over time but that consumption habits did not. In order to obtain greater stability, therefore, planners who excluded rationing would either have to induce rapid fluctuation in saving habits, of just the right degree, or else they must seek in some way to "smooth out" investment demand.

It was felt that in a free society comprehensive planning could undoubtedly affect the long run proportion of saving, but that it was very doubtful if the marginal and average saving responses of free human beings could be influenced fast enough and accurately enough to ensure cyclical stability. The government could probably *reduce* spending fairly well, but to induce rapid increases and then decreases, in a wealthy economy, would appear attendant with almost insuperable difficulties. What is needed is not high saving or low saving but variable saving—variable in just the right amount. It seemed likely, therefore, that the planners would try, instead, to smooth out investment demand at a rate consistent with the long run proportion of saving they have selected or ascertained. But could the job be done?

A great deal depended upon the condition of the economy when the planners took over. There are many economists who view the business cycle in terms of preventing the boom. Such a point of view appears tacitly based on the assumption that after each disturbance the system returns to an "equilibrium" with full employment. If this were true socialism could probably furnish the necessary negative planning, but, as we saw, even then only at the expense of making the consumer wait.

Another group recognizes that, in a society which has experienced many booms, the capital and durable goods industries are "permanently" "over" built relative to the rest of the economy. In that case, even if there were no drop in demand for consumer's goods, the end of a boom would find unemployed men and resources in the capital and durable goods industries.

But many such writers feel that there is some average rate of expansion at which the system can be stabilized, or some point, for example the "inflection" point, at which the expansion should be stopped. If socialism could find this rate, or this point, it may be said, all would be well. From such an opinion the writer dissents. It may always be granted that vigorous rationing, prolonged public works, and retardation of innovation can smooth out an expansion. But parties advocating comprehensive planning do not campaign, "Elect us and we will ration for years, hold back new inventions perhaps still longer, keep you on public works and the dole in the interval, and, in return give you—stability." Not at all. The promise is to give and invent things for the consumer "bigger and better" and faster than under capitalism—and give nearly perfect stability.

This promise, it seems to me, sets up contradictory standards which cannot possibly all be met simultaneously by mere anticipatory planning, however perfect. We cannot run a line through the "average" of a cycle and call that "equilibrium"— for to do so leaves many unemployed. But on the other hand if we expand too rapidly, so as to get full employment, we are almost sure to entail eventual waste, or depression, or unemployment. This is true whether we can forecast the market pattern of wants or not, for the problem does not concern *amount* but *speed*. To put the difficulty in a nutshell: *The socially tolerable rate of expansion likely to be demanded in a democratic society will probably be much faster than the "equi-*

librium" rate which would ensure a permanent full employment adjustment.

Even if we knew what the eventual "perfect" adjustment could be, the rapidly growing organism would distort itself in getting there. Even if we finally achieved an adjustment, each great new invention would raise the problem anew of how to satisfy the consumer *promptly* and yet maintain stability.

The conclusion to which we are driven is that no amount of comprehensive *ex ante* planning, which also wished to give the consumer *what* he wanted *when* he wanted it, could succeed in smoothing out the aggregate demand for investment. Inevitably the policy which it would be led to adopt (assuming that a really *bona fide* effort is made to meet the consumer) is the despised capitalist policy of compensatory public works, etc. In other words the inevitable discontinuities of rapid capitalist growth would remain inevitable in rapid socialist growth, but, during the intervals between bursts, the planners could organize various social desires for durable goods to fill in the gap. Compensatory policy then is not a mere crutch for a decadent capitalism. It is an essential safety precaution for any rapidly growing society genuinely seeking to satisfy the consumer.

The writer does not wish to give the impression that such compensatory policy is not filled with difficulty, and that it does not entail numerous problems of its own. There is a very large literature on the subject and the present volume is not primarily concerned with remedies but with diagnosis. However, it should be clear that an intelligent capitalist democracy could also make use of such measures and that the difference between it and the comprehensively planned state, in this regard, becomes not one of kind so much as of degree. We shall return to this problem in the next chapter.

Finally it is submitted that our analysis suggests the conclusion that the instability of capitalism, and its "over" expansion of the durable goods industries, is not so much the result of the specific capitalist framework as of the democratic and liberal values. Precisely because competitive capitalism working through the profit motive still rushes forward, to a considerable extent, to satisfy changes in consumer's demand *promptly*—precisely for that reason it is unstable. Omnipotent, omniscient planning eliminates many subordinate difficulties but a basic dilemma remains. A socialism accepting the same basic values regarding the consumer would encounter much the same problem and be forced to employ much the same remedies. The problem concerns not so much "planning" versus non-planning, as rationing *versus* speed.

CHAPTER VII

SOME FUNCTIONAL ASPECTS OF THE MODERN CRISIS

So far we have traced only the cyclical consequences of the failure of consumption habits and investment to adjust themselves spontaneously in a rapidly growing society. Now we must consider some of the secular effects, and examine the problem of "long run" unemployment.

Throughout our study we have used an analytical schema intended to supplement rather than contradict that of Lord Keynes, and the same will be true of the present chapter.[1] The Keynesian analysis of the causes of secular unemployment in the United States and Western Europe during the 1930's is accepted *in toto*—but with an important qualification. Granted that there will be trouble if the inducement to invest drops off without a corresponding rise in the propensity to consume. Granted the bad effects of "liquidity preference" in maintaining the rate of interest in the face of a falling marginal efficiency of capital. But why does the *long run* marginal efficiency of capital fall?

The usual explanation in terms of secular maldistribution of wealth or declining rates of growth of population in the West do not appear to the writer very convincing. This does not imply a denial of the importance of population growth to investment. It is only that there seem ample poverty and population in the world—notably Asia—to absorb all our investment. Nor need this be said reasoning in terms of necessity alone, but also

---

[1] The relation between my views and those of Lord Keynes is given in my "Future of Keynesian Economics," *American Economic Review*, June, 1945.

in terms of need *relative to* the secular propensity to consume. The spark submitted to be lacking is foreign trade and foreign investment.[2]

Everyone will admit that the obstacles to a reorganization of large scale capitalist international lending are very great. But even some of the more extreme stagnationists appear grudgingly compelled to admit that such difficulties ultimately reduce very largely to an intensely hostile ideological climate.[3] Were it not for this ideological hostility the inducement to invest at the present time would rise rapidly. With rapidly increasing investment, relative to consumption, unemployment would begin to disappear. The *secular* propensity to consume schedule seems to rise of itself. Nobody supposes that thereafter all could be smooth sailing, but the cycle is a different problem from long range stagnation. Our task here will be to inquire into some of the reasons why such a hostile ideology has arisen. Like Professor Schumpeter, though for rather different reasons, the writer believes that capitalism is an organism which may turn out to be killing itself through the generation of a milieu unfavorable to its own survival.

Through our work so far we have tried to avoid, as much as possible, any reference to specific capitalist institutional peculiarities. We have referred, in the main, merely to societies which used money, consulted the consumer, and were expanding. In the matter of secular stagnation, however, it is necessary to make an excursion into more definitely capitalist phenomena.

Everyone—socialist, fascist, or capitalist—will agree that the capitalist era has been one of extraordinarily rapid growth. The admission can be made quite irrespective of one's opinion concerning how much better a job socialism could or could not do. Yet it is submitted that the coincidence of scientific growth,

[2] Cf., my "Hopes and Fears—the Shape of Things to Come," *Review of Economic Statistics*, Vol. XXVI, No. 4, November, 1944, p. 206; "The Great Guessing Game—Terborgh vs. Hansen," *Review of Economic Statistics*, February, 1946.
[3] Cf., Alan Sweezy, "Secular Stagnation," in *Post-War Economic Problems*, ed. S. E. Harris (New York, McGraw-Hill Book Company, Inc., 1943), p. 80, note.

expansion, and capitalism is not accidental but arises from certain intrinsic peculiarities of the capitalist framework itself.

It would seem that these peculiarities, as the writer has argued at length elsewhere,[4] center around the existence of a largely unregulated but vigorous competition—not necessarily either "pure" or "perfect" but, as J. M. Clark puts it, "workable." Social progress, in the sense of technical change, and a rising output per head, would seem to depend upon how the balance of power lies between those whose interests are best served by maintaining the *status quo* and those who stand most to gain by change. Now in the stringently planned and regulated cultures —which constitute by far the greater portion of recorded civilizations—the administration of a country has tended to be in the hands of *self-perpetuating* elites. Only in times of war, upheaval or social disturbance has the group in power been appreciably invaded without its own consent. Yet cultural history certainly indicates that self-perpetuating groups tend to narrow themselves. The agreeable conformist is preferred to the man with a new idea and the too eager inquirer is constantly in danger of being burnt at the stake or otherwise "liquidated." It is in disturbed times that the new idea and the new man have had a chance, and this phenomenon probably underlies Professor Whitehead's observation in *Science and the Modern World* that "on the whole the great ages have been unstable ages."

Capitalism, however, has been an extremely unstable system for reasons which we have already seen. Furthermore, especially in the United States, there have been few upper classes in history more open to invasion from below. A competitive rather than a customary market, and the introduction of technical change, has constantly made possible the rise of new commercial dynasties, while the rise of new commercial dynasties, by preventing the social pattern from freezing, has equally constantly facilitated technical change and kept the social pattern from becoming unduly rigid.

[4] Cf., my "Business and the Radical Indictment," *Harvard Business Review*, Summer, 1945. Also my "Hopes and Fears," above note 2.

Yet the sum total of this process of rapid growth and change has been intense social strain. There has been a tremendous amount of individual insecurity. The constant changes of an advancing science have raised some to affluence while plunging others to poverty; have left one region stranded while raising others to great wealth, and all with staggering rapidity. These results we have seen follow also, to a considerable extent, for rapidly growing socialisms as well as capitalisms, but in either case the social frictions can be tremendous, increasing in intensity with the speed of the whole process.

It has, therefore, taken a very strong and deeply ingrained ideology to persuade the people to accept such constant drastic disturbance. The capitalist ideology has been the gospel of *laissez faire*—the undoubtedly correct idea that in a growing market economy individual insecurity might be mitigated, but not prevented; and the much more questionable one that for society as a whole the working of competition would serve to adjust the total of change so as best to promote the public good. There was a time when the classical economists had very nearly converted the whole Western world to this view.

Unfortunately, as we have seen, for reasons which, as far as stability goes, need have no essential connection with capitalism *but* with rapid growth; the doctrine of self-adjustment and the "invisible hand" has been progressively discredited. The impact of depression upon an increasingly rootless and urbanized population has been ever more severe. Today the circumstances of our life make us far more impressed with present insecurity than long-run growth.

As a result all sorts of non- or anti-capitalist ideas have obtained increasing authority. All strike at the idea of competition and through it—if the writer's point of view be accepted—at the idea of unregulated access to the top, and hence—again supposing one to accept the author's idea of the deterioration and hardening of the self-perpetuating elite—at the institutional peculiarity making for long-run rapid growth and change. However unconsciously, the present movement to *plan* change and growth is in many of its forms really a movement to end change and growth.

There is an anti-capitalism of the right and of the left. Radical anti-capitalism we may put aside for the present. What we need to do here is to consider some of the reasons for the increasing distrust of competition which underlies conservative anti-capitalism, and which is best summed up in the slogan, "cut-throat" competition. It is a curious paradox that despite the fact that numerous surveys have shown that economics of "large scale production" stop far short of the "monopoly" point, in many industries, nevertheless, the movement for the concentration of industry appears often still to go on. Is the matter one of mere megalomania? It is submitted that our cycle theory contains an element which may be of value in solving this paradox.

(1) Speed, Growth and "Cut-throat" Competition

The phrase "cut-throat" competition may be most respectably and charitably defined as competition resulting in a price below the long run *real* costs of production.[5] It is submitted that, taken in that sense, pure competition under the "normal" conditions of a rapidly growing world is almost bound to be cut-throat.[6] From this there arises a well-nigh insoluble dilemma of trade regulation.

The long-run real costs of an industry, in any society, are depreciation and (if there is change) obsolescence. Depending upon one's economic predilections one can add interest, "reasonable" profit, amortization and so on. Since a discussion of the social necessity of profit, interest, etc., is not immediately necessary to our exposition we may leave it to one side and discuss depreciation alone.

[5] In this sense it closely resembles Marshall's "spoiling the market."

[6] Using Chamberlin's distinction between "pure" competition in the sense of the elasticity of the individual demand curve and "perfect" competition in the sense of a "frictionless" market. The *durability* of equipment might be called a "friction" or an "imperfection." Hence a market could be called "pure" at the same time that it was not "perfect."

It is usually said that purely competitive price equals marginal or prime cost. But does marginal or prime cost include depreciation? I believe the most usual answer is no.

Such a reply is generally based upon a tacit acceptance of Alfred Marshall's short-run theory of value in which it is supposed that the long-run costs need not be covered in the "short run" because fixed equipment may be taken as given. But Marshall's theory in this connection is either wrong or else contains an important tacit assumption.[7] For if the capital equipment of an industry has been built up *gradually* so as to wear out *in a steady stream*, the real long-run costs would be nearly as immediately pressing in the short run, and under pure competition, as the short-run costs.

Suppose that the equilibrium market demand for a product is one hundred units a year and that to produce one hundred units, ten plants are needed. Suppose further that one plant wears out each year. If that were the case, and even leaving aside profits, etc., a short-run cost which failed to cover depreciation would almost immediately be rectified.[8] For under such circumstances, if each plant is independent and competing, and supposing no fortuitous accumulation of an extra "war chest," the firm whose plant has worn out, but which does not have adequate funds available for replacement, would have to close down. Supply would be curtailed relatively soon and competitive price forced up once more to the "proper" level. Even in Dr. Lange's competitive socialism the trust which did not make its depreciation might lose out unless specially subsidized.

It follows from the example just given that Marshall's theory of short-run value may be interpreted as a tacit rationalization of pricing in the trough of a replacement "wave." The long-run

[7] I do not mean to say that Marshall himself did not understand the proper nature of the case. I am only pointing out that to stop the clock as he does for his short-run period is an extremely unrealistic assumption—except that it happens to fit the real *cyclical* world!

[8] How long the process would take would depend upon the proportion borne by the output of the individual plant being retired to the total output of the "industry."

costs (however defined) may, broadly speaking, be ignored in the short run only if the age distribution of the life span of the machinery of the competing firms is not "normal."

However, *abnormal* age distribution of durable goods is exactly what our theory would lead us to expect. Were expansion to take place at the "Equilibrium" rate spoken of in the last chapter, cut-throat competition, as we have defined it, would be well-nigh impossible. But *rapid* satisfaction of consumer's wants means the *simultaneous* erection of many durable plants, means the *over* building of the durable goods industries, means eventual cut-throat competition in the consumer's goods industries, if not elsewhere as well, and finally means pressures toward monopolistic "rationalization."

We may conclude that the practical instinct of the businessman in distrusting pure competition is quite sound, however much the academic economist may scold. Under the conditions usually found in our rapidly and discontinuously growing modern world, pure competition is only too often likely to mean industrial suicide. We may therefore conclude that our theory suggests that the decisive advantage of "monopoly" or coöperating oligopoly, so far as explaining their survival is concerned, is *superior ability to stabilize the market after a rapid expansion*. And we may further conclude that cases can be set up in which the exercise of such a "monopoly" power could be quite defensible.

But—and here is the dilemma for trade regulation—this doctrine, though valid, is nevertheless intensely dangerous. For few are so naive as to suppose that voluntary price setting would necessarily stop at the social optimum. Furthermore, it is hard to distinguish between illegitimate price cutting, and the lower price of the man with a new idea and new equipment. Only too often coöperative ethics and oligopolistic stabilization are the forerunner of the "Dead hand," and the end of technical progress. In the same way the idea of slowing down expansion to avoid a slump is equally valid, and equally dangerous. For the emphasis is apt to be on the slow-down rather than the eventual purpose, and so it too may become the justification of all sorts of practices retarding national wealth. Yet in both these cases a program of "filling in" to smooth out capital demand furnishes some amelioration. For if it were followed we could be less afraid of letting the expansion go ahead. And also by removing severe deflationary pressure much of the urge toward "cut-throat" competition would be avoided. The "first degree of monopoly"—as some have called it—i.e., the mere recognition of mutual inter-dependence might serve to keep price cutting within bounds without creating a socially intolerable degree of "monopoly" power, and without too completely closing the door to change and the new idea.

(2) The Security Economy

With the analysis of cut-throat competition and consequent pressure toward monopoly and oligopoly, we have completed our survey of the specific relationship of the theory of our earlier chapters with the ideas which tend to discredit the working of the capitalist order, and undermine its ideology. And we have seen how inevitably the matter traces back to the fact of rapid growth. The organism, in the very act of growing, almost inevitably distorts itself. From the scientific change and progress which are our pride come the insecurity and unemployment which are our curse.

But one more factor need be mentioned as contributing to secular stagnation and that is the pressure group problem. When the cells of the human body set up business on their own and prey upon the remainder, we call it a cancer. When the same thing happens in the economic body we may call it a monopoly—or we may call it patriotic protection, or a trade institute, or an N.I.R.A., or a trade union.[9] And such is our semantic hypnosis that the change of label makes all the difference in the world. Yet, however high flown the label, an economic body which has accumulated a sufficiency of these can-

[9] Which is not, of course, to call all trade unions "cancers" any more than it is to brand all trade institutes by that name.

cers must stop. Nationalism, restrictive trade unionism, monopoly, all are the outgrowth of a refusal of the parts to yield to the whole. All derive increasing prestige from the instability of the system, and in the end their joint action, unless checked, will destroy the system. It follows that rapid growth, with its attendant instability, fosters the growth of the very forces which in the end will bring it to a close. For instability increases the tendency to associate in pressure groups. It is to this process, and its many other attendant anti-capitalist ideas, that the writer attributes the decline in the marginal efficiency of capital which is the ultimate explanation of secular (as distinguished from cyclical) unemployment.[10] It is not that capitalism today is potentially any less useful than it was before. It is simply that the area of economic life, and world geography, in which the effects of competition and consequent rapid growth are tolerated, is being progressively limited.

CONCLUSION

Yet once more we are left with the question: Can "planning" solve the problem. Can it do a better job of obtaining security than capitalism, and yet retain that rapid growth and relative freedom of access to the top which have been among the chief justifications of a vigorous capitalism? [11] The answer, it is submitted, depends upon what we mean by "planning." If the word planning means the comprehensive licensing and control of all industrial growth by some central planning board, and if sole reliance is to be placed upon *ex ante* direction of invest-

[10] Cf., the articles mentioned *supra*, note 2.

[11] Note the adjective *vigorous* applied to capitalism. When capitalism—merely defined as the existence of private property—has been in a prolonged slump through a combination of hostility and bad policy—as in England—private business comes to exhibit all the characteristics of the deteriorating "self-perpetuating" elite already mentioned. And so it often happens that the very people of unusual energy and vision who would normally be finding their way to the top in industry, are so discouraged or repelled that they devote their energies instead to the overthrow of the system. It is a curious paradox that under this condition, the type of man—the natural rebel and inquirer—who would be most unhappy in a mature socialism, with its frozen pattern and unquestioned orthodoxy, is the very man who in the initial stages derives most satisfaction from creating socialism.

ment to avoid disturbance, then our analysis shows that *all* the values sought to be realized cannot, in the nature of things, be satisfied simultaneously.

If the fundamental fabric of this book has any validity at all, the fundamental devil, regarding instability, is not capitalism but rapid growth. There is an inexorable conflict between giving the consumer what he wants *when* he wants it and complete planned stability. If complete stability be our end, therefore, planning will not do the job—if we apply the liberal values. What is needed in such a case is not planning to express the liberal values but planning to destroy them. Stop growth and science, or slow them down tremendously. Make the consumer wait or take what you give him. These are the real requirements —and the debate over "planning" versus "capitalism" a sham battle. In any society the ultimate price of complete social stability and security is stagnation.

But there is another meaning of planning and that is a planning which attempts merely to "fill in" and prevent severe deflation. Such planning can never produce as perfect stability as the other and the greater the perfection demanded of it the more it merges into a general system of centralized control. Yet it is not futile. For could one achieve an ideological reconstruction of capitalism—showing its connection with democracy and science—and thus obtain a removal of many of the fetters now binding the system; could one then keep deflation and unemployment within bounds; the way would once more be open to a wider freedom and a renewed achievement—and many of the evils we have been discussing would be greatly ameliorated even though not totally removed.

For example, in the case of monopoly, and the bunching of capital goods demand, maintenance of tolerable stability by a judicious use of public works and purchasing power stabilization schemes would mitigate as we have already seen the pressures toward an unsocial price cutting, and, by permitting a spontaneously smoother introduction of new invention, would help the "waves" of capital installation to disintegrate. Truly liberal planned socialism, we have seen, could not do much more.

The real obstacle to such a policy, however, is a psychological one. For it remains to be seen whether we can raise the slogans of stability and security to the pitch we have done and not cast the balance irrevocably in favor of the vested interest,[12] the dead hand, and eventual stagnation.

The primary concern of the present volume is with diagnosis. The writer does not mean to say that the considerations he has adduced are conclusive regarding final social choice. There are many other ends beside scientific progress. It is believed and hoped that the analysis here presented will be useful to a comprehensively planned state as well as to a relatively stabilized democratic capitalism. I hope to present in a later book the philosophic and aesthetic reasoning which impels me to prefer the latter system.

But if personal opinion may be briefly intruded, I should like to sum up my own conclusion regarding the nature of the modern crisis: I believe that much of the insecurity and the instability which we now decry is the result of the scientific achievement and the social democracy which we admire. But our profound malaise is ignorant, blind, and only semiconscious. The full accumulated bitterness and resentment of all the groups who are inconvenienced or losing ground is being discharged not at science and democracy but, under high-flown labels, at the capitalistic order in the name of science and democracy. On these terms the present volume is not intended to dictate our choice, but it is hoped that it will help us to make it a bit more intelligently.

[12] The "vested interest" may mean the vested interest of the bureaucrat in his job, as well as the capitalist in his dividends. Cf., my articles, notes 2 and 4.

APPENDIX ON INCOME FLOW AND PRICES

(1) An Act of Saving versus a Flow

As long as one considers an act of saving in isolation, or in an economy in which saving has not previously been occurring, it is easy to demonstrate that maladjustment is likely to result. The point is illustrated in Figure A which is the basic figure of this appendix.

As in Chapter I we assume to begin with:

I. Full employment.

II. Only three types of goods: (a) a single homogeneous "single use" commodity called a "consumer's good"; (b) machinery and equipment used in the process of production; (c) a floating mass of "single use" raw materials and semi-finished goods on its way toward being made up either into machinery and equipment or else consumer's goods.

III. "Linear" production of intermediate goods—i.e., "loops" and "whirlpools" are omitted or ignored.

To these we add:

IV. No changes in the market consumption patterns or in technique.

V. No change in population.

VI. Machinery and equipment must be manufactured in the first instance but thereafter lasts forever.

VII. Only two types of business unit exist. These are (a) concerns making consumer's goods and all the raw materials, etc., going into them save machinery and equipment; (b) concerns making machinery and equipment and the raw materials, etc., going into them. In this way the intermediate stages of production in types (a) and (b) appear only as labor costs. Money is therefore used only to pay wages and to purchase final consumption goods and machinery and equipment. At any one period of time only a fraction of the wage bill of types (a) and (b) will be paid with reference to men working on the actual completion of the product.

99

VIII. Only labor costs are considered—depreciation, profits, interest, etc., are ignored.

IX. We assume a finite but relatively short period of time to be called a "day," so chosen that no unit of money can be exchanged in it more than once against "output"—that is to say against consumer's goods and machinery and equipment.

This concept is of course derived from Professor Robertson though my "day" is a little different from his.

X. For the present, bank credit is ruled out and the quantity of money is taken as fixed.

XI. Consumer's goods are assumed to be made in one "day" for the sale the next "day."

XII. Wages in the consumer's goods industries are paid at the commencement of each "day" either from funds earned by the sale of consumer's goods "yesterday" or money borrowed for the purpose "today." They are paid with reference to consumer's goods being made "today" for sale "tomorrow."

XIII. "Disposable" wages "today," that is to say, those wages concerning which the choice is made "today" between spending and saving, are the wages paid "yesterday." Thus, in a typical case, money is earned by a concern from the sale of goods on "Monday," is paid to workers on "Tuesday," and may be spent or saved by them on "Wednesday."

XIV. Money "saved" is money retained "today" from "today's" "disposable" wages.

XV. Money saved "today" is assumed always to be transferred "today" to a concern which makes machinery and equipment. This concern then uses the money "tomorrow" to pay workers in making machinery and equipment "tomorrow" which will be delivered to a new customer's goods concern and put into operation "day after tomorrow."

The problem of selecting an appropriate time sequence for saving and investment proved a serious one. It is tempting to assume that money saved "today" is used "today" to purchase completed machinery and equipment. Such an assumption avoids a host of difficulties. But where would the machinery and equipment come from? Each act of saving would have to be anticipated a "day" in advance by the machine makers. This is not far from what actually happens in a continuing system but in showing the effects of changes in saving, or Mr. Durbin's "beginning of saving," it slurs over the process by which men and resources are transferred from consumer's goods manufacture into making machinery and equipment.

A similar difficulty appears in assuming that savings "today" are used "today" in employing men in making machinery and equipment for delivery "tomorrow." Where are the men coming from to make the machines? Remember that we have assumed full employment and that the consumer's goods industries have, as yet, had nothing to disturb them or to induce them to contract. The only possible source of labor is an increase in the population. See XVI below. This, indeed, will be considered later on.

Some may also object to making the time of production of machinery and equipment equal to the time of production of a consumer's good. This is unrealistic but it is useful as a matter of preliminary convenience. Changing it would greatly increase the difficulty of the problem. This will be indicated later on in applying our model.

Finally problems are raised as to where the machine makers get the money to pay their workers. Bank credit to begin with is ruled out, yet if the makers of machinery are not paid until their product is completed they must work a "day" without pay. For all these reasons it seemed best to assume initially that the makers of machinery unlike the makers of consumer's goods, were paid in advance.

XVI. Factor combinations are unalterable.

XVII. The marginal propensity to consume unless otherwise noted is unity.

We are now in a position to consider Figure A. We start in Day I in a stationary state or "circular flow." Only a single corporation exists which makes consumer's goods, and semi-finished goods, as outlined in assumption VII. We call this corporation O—the "original" corporation. The wage bill is $1,000,000, and hence by assumption VIII the price of the "daily" output of consumer's goods is $1,000,000. By way of simplification we assume, to begin with, a one for one relationship between consumer's goods, men, and money. Thus in any one "day" there are assumed to be one million men receiving one million dollars and producing, in the aggregate, one million consumer's goods each of which costs $1.00. Through this assumption we are able to relate wages, men and the money supply. From assumption IX through XIII, and an examination of the

FIGURE A (Chapter II)

	Day I "O"	Day II "O"	Day III "O"	Day IV "O"	Day V "O"
Goods being made: quantity	1,000,000	1,000,000	800,000	1,000,000	1,000,000
value	$1,000,000	$1,000,000	$800,000	$1,000,000	$1,000,000 or $1,250,000
Goods on sale: quantity	1,000,000	1,000,000	1,000,000	800,000	1,000,000
value	$1,000,000	$1,000,000	$1,000,000 or $800,000	$800,000	$1,000,000 or $1,250,000
Number of men employed	1,000,000	1,000,000	800,000	1,000,000	1,000,000
wages paid	$1,000,000	$1,000,000	$800,000	$1,000,000	$1,000,000
wages "disposable"	$1,000,000	$1,000,000	$1,000,000	$800,000	$1,000,000
wages spent	$1,000,000	$800,000	$1,000,000	$800,000	$1,000,000
wages saved		$200,000			
Gross receipts at end of period	$1,000,000	$200,000 "M"	$1,000,000 "M"	$1,000,000	$1,000,000
Goods being made: quantity			100,000		
value			$200,000		
Goods on sale: quantity				200,000	
value				$200,000	
Number of men employed			200,000		
wages paid			$200,000		
wages "disposable"					
wages spent					
wages saved					
Gross receipts at end of period		$200,000	$200,000		
Goods being made: quantity				"E"	"E" 200,000
value					$200,000 or $250,000
Goods on sale: quantity					200,000
value					$200,000 or $250,000
Number of men employed				200,000	200,000
wages paid				$200,000 (borrowed)	$200,000 (borrowed)
wages "disposable"					$200,000
wages spent					$200,000
wages saved					
Gross receipts at end of period					
Total Goods on Sale	$1,000,000	$1,000,000	$800,000 or $1,000,000	$800,000	$1,200,000 or $1,500,000
Total Wages Spent	$1,000,000	$800,000	$1,000,000	$1,000,000	$1,200,000
Price per unit	$1.00	80¢	$1.00	$1.25	$1.00
		Loss $200,000	Possible "Gain" $200,000	Gain $200,000	Possible "loss" $250,000 no further borrowing needed

102

FIGURE B (Chapter II)

	Days I & II "O"	Day III "O"	Day IV "O"	Day V "O"	Day VI "O"
Goods being made: quantity	Same as Figure A	800,000	800,000	Same as Day IV	Same as Day IV
value		$800,000	$800,000		
Goods on sale: quantity		1,000,000	800,000		
value		$1,000,000 or $800,000	$800,000		
Number of men employed		800,000	800,000		
wages paid		$800,000	$800,000		
wages "disposable"		$1,000,000	$800,000		
wages spent		$800,000	$600,000		
wages saved		$200,000	$200,000		
Gross receipts at end of period		$800,000	$800,000		
	"M"	"M"	"M"	"M"	"M"
Goods being made: quantity	Same as Figure A	100,000	100,000	Same as Day IV	Same as Day IV
value		$200,000	$200,000		
Goods on sale: quantity			100,000		
value			$200,000		
Number of men employed		200,000	200,000		
wages paid		$200,000	$200,000		
wages "disposable"			$200,000		
wages spent			$200,000		
wages saved					
Gross receipts at end of period			$200,000		
			"E'"	"E"	"E" Same as Day V But no more loans needed
Goods being made: quantity			200,000	200,000	
value			$200,000	$200,000	
Goods on sale: quantity				200,000	
value				$200,000	
Number of men employed			200,000	200,000	
wages paid			$200,000 (borrowed)	$200,000 (borrowed)	
wages "disposable"				$200,000	
wages spent				$200,000	
wages saved					
Gross receipts at end of period				$200,000	
				"E'" Same as E' in Day IV	"E'" Same as E' in Day V
					"E''" Same as E'' in Day V
Total Goods on Sale		$800,000	$800,000	$1,000,000	$1,200,000
Total Wages Spent		$800,000	$800,000	$1,000,000	$1,200,000
Price per unit		$1.00	$1.00	$1.00	$1.00

figure the reader will deduce that the quantity of money is $2,000,000, the transaction's velocity of circulation unity, the "circuit" velocity ½.

Let us now assume that in Day II the workers save from their "disposable" wages $200,000 and transfer it to a corporation to be called M which has been organized to make machinery and equipment. The time sequence of this transaction has been set out in assumption XV. Since the money spent on consumer's goods in Day II will now only be $800,000, O will not be able to sell all its output at a dollar per unit and will take a loss of $200,000. We assume that O disposes of its entire output, however, at a price of 80 cents but decides to curtail production in the next period to 800,000 units of consumer's goods and thus avoid losses and return to the old price level. In consequence at the end of Day II, 200,000 men are dismissed.

But at the beginning of Day III M is starting operations and will be able to employ some, or all, of these men. Thus the losses in O have, indeed, disturbed O, but they have had a useful function to perform in inducing O to contract and *set men free* for new investment. Without this release of men by O it would be *impossible*, under our assumptions, to make the new investment. Let us now assume that M reemploys all 200,000 men with the $200,000 it received in the previous period from the savers, and uses them to make $200,000 worth of machinery and equipment. At the end of Day III this equipment is delivered to a corporation E which hopes to use it to expand the output of consumer's goods, and which expects to start operation in Day IV.

Meanwhile, before discussing Day IV, we must see what has been going on with O. O has cut the number of goods *being made* in Day III to 800,000 but goods *on sale* in Day III are 1,000,000 for they were made "yesterday," before the decision was taken to curtail production. "Disposable" wages in Day III are also $1,000,000 for while 200,000 men were dismissed by O at the end of Day II they each had a day's pay in their hands at the time, which, by definition, could not be "disposed" until Day III. These men are all now working for M and hence have no reason not to spend. Since we assume that there is no further saving O can now once more sell 1,000,000 goods for $1,000,000 and the old price level is restored.

It would be natural, therefore, for O to wish to return to its old level of production, or even to expand it but if it tries to do so there will be a labor shortage and a general deadlock. Corporation M, to be sure, will go out of business for there is no further demand for its services. There are thus available 200,000 men to be returned to consumer's goods production. But since the total labor force is only 1,000,000 men and O wants to use all of them, E cannot get any labor to operate its new machines. E, however, is also in a bad way financially for the savers have spent all their money on machinery and equipment and have left nothing over for E's operating expenses.

Let us, however, consider the case which the underconsumptionists usually have in mind and remove assumptions V and X. The population is then allowed to increase to permit 200,000 new men to grow up to operate E's plant, and a bank is also added, but this bank is assumed never to call a loan and charges no interest. It would seem that on these highly favorable assumptions further trouble would be avoided but such is not necessarily the case. In Day IV the increase in the labor force is matched by a loan of $200,000 to E by the bank. Reference to the figure will show that wages disposable in Day IV will be $1,000,000, but goods on sales will be only 800,000. There will therefore be a profit to O of $200,000 and a rise in the price level of consumer's goods from 100 to 125.

Now O may simply see that gross receipts have not increased and hence keep prices in Day V at 100, or $1,000,000 for 1,000,000 goods. E will put an additional 200,000 consumer's goods on the market but this will be matched by the $200,000 additional disposable wages of the new men which E borrowed in Day IV. E will also borrow another $200,000 to meet its current pay roll in Day V. Since, however, no attempt is being made to recover depreciation costs, etc., no further borrowing by E is needed and we have arrived at a new equilibrium in which $1,200,000 worth of consumer's goods will be met each day by $1,200,000 worth of disposable wages. This is the most favorable result. On the other hand O may try to maintain the new price level of 125 and E may also make the attempt. In that case expectations will be sadly disappointed for the goods will be priced at $1,500,000 but the available disposable wages will be but $1,200,000.

We may thus conclude that, in our model, even under very favorable assumptions a single act of saving considered in isolation or a temporary increase in the amount of saving in an economy where saving has not been occurring, will be likely to induce the following disturbances: (1) losses in the consumer's goods industries and a fall in their price level; (2) a rise in the price level of consumer's goods as the money reappears in expenditure on machinery and equipment. This expansion may indeed actually pass through a temporary equilibrium of consumer's goods prices and incomes at the old price level; (3) a fall in the price level of consumer's goods as increased output appears.

Other sequences may be developed showing different relative and absolute changes in the price level of consumer's goods but in all of them the *direction* of price movement is likely to be the same. Among possible assumptions we may mention, in particular, the case in which the savers spend only a fraction of money on machinery and equipment and keep enough on hand to provide for operating expenses. This involves a change in the velocity of money. The results will be (a) if the population does not increase, a new eventual equilibrium in which the old working force is shared between O and E. The new saving will have been abortive, however, for the added machinery cannot be used. Under our assumptions, indeed, it cannot possibly be used unless more men are added. (b) If new men are added, but the money supply is not increased, a new equilibrium will be reached in which output will have expanded but a lower price and wage level will prevail. But in either case the sequence of price movement: fall, rise, and fall again will be the same. So much of the underconsumptionist thesis, under our severe assumptions, is correct.

We shall now, however, consider the effect not of a single act of saving, or a temporary change in the amount saved, but an act of saving which is part of a *steady flow* of savings whose absolute amount does not change. This is shown in Figure B. To begin let us return to assumptions I through XVII above. Days I and II are the same as in Figure A. In Day III, however, the men employed in O again save $200,000 and transfer it to M as per assumption XV. Thus disposable wages spent and prices do not rise in Day III in Figure B as they did in Figure A. In Day IV we have the same impasse we found in Figure A and we avoid it in the same way by relaxing assumptions V and X and allowing the population and the quantity of money to increase. As an inspection of Figure B will show, a new expanding equilibrium is attained after Day IV. The population, the quantity of money and the output of consumer's goods will all rise by 200,000 units each "day," and there will be no further changes in the price level. We thus see that an act of saving which is part of a steady flow need not always, by itself, cause any disturbance of employment, prices or production.

In a *single* act of saving in an economy in which saving has not been occurring there is a real disturbance. Men, if we assume full employment and unchanged technique, must be transferred from the consumer's goods industries, to the making of machines, and then back again. The three changes of the price level spoken of above reflect these three stages of the "real" process. But when there is a constant amount of saving per period there is no real disturbance. Corporation M—the machine maker—remains always of the same size and once the appropriate figure has been reached no further transfer is necessary.

If, as under our assumptions, bank credit is increasing in the proper manner, then income, population, the output of consumer's goods, and the money supply all rise *pari passu*. Each individual act of saving does *not* cause a shortage of consumer purchasing power. Indeed each act of saving is essential to monetary equilibrium for without it there would be a price inflation and an attempt to switch men away from the making of machinery and equipment. If bank credit is not increased there will be no "real" disturbance, but there will be a falling price level of consumer's goods.

Before closing this section we have one more task to perform— What if there be not a constant amount of saving but a constant percent of saving? In that case as disposable wages rise the *amount* of savings increases though the proportion saved will not. Some very curious results follow under the assumptions used in Figure B. For in Figure B each sum disbursed by the machine makers is of a size equal to the saving of the *previous* period. Now if a constant percentage rather than a constant amount be used, then, as disposable wages increase, the savings in each "day" will be larger in *absolute* amount than the savings of the day before, and wages in Corporation M will not emerge in a sufficient quantity. Wages in M, so to speak, will always be one lap behind and hence the price level must slowly fall—and this even though the banks lend to the consumer's goods corporations as outlined in Figure B.

Even this curious dilemma can be overcome by varying our assumptions yet again. Let us assume that every act of saving is anticipated a "day" in advance by the makers of machinery, the growth in the population, and by the banks, also that the banks lend to the machine makers for operating expenses (wages) as well as to consumer's goods corporations. Under these assumptions there need never be any drop in the price level. These assumptions are not far off reality for a continuing system which is smoothly expanding. In the case, however, of an unexpected change in saving they appear too easy. Another remarkable result entailed is that if we assume a constant percentage of income saved then the *absolute* growth of population, output, and money, in equilibrium, will take the form of a *compound interest curve*. We conclude therefore that the case of a constant proportion saved raises special difficulties not found when savings are only of a constant amount. But the conclusions as to an absolute amount remain valid, and it is apparent that not every act of saving will cause a disturbance and "shortage."

(2) Debt Repayment

So far the effect of a repayment of bank credit has been dodged and the point must now be specifically considered. As we saw in Figure B a constant flow of saving implies a constantly falling price level unless bank credit and the money supply be expanded. It follows that it will not be sufficient, in an expanding society, for the banks simply to re-lend what is paid back to them. They must also maintain their *net* new injection of purchasing power. But we cannot always assume that the banks will be able to get just the required amount of money into circulation.

Let us suppose first that we have the conditions shown in Figure B. There is full employment and the banking system is of the old fashioned "orthodox" "commercial" type. Bank loans are only made for short terms on inventory, etc., and not for fixed capital purposes. Suppose now in Day IV of Figure B corporation E^1 repays a $200,000 loan. It would be extremely difficult, if not impossible, in our model, for E^1 to do this without curtailing its operations, or those of someone else, but let us skip this difficulty. The bank will now have $200,000 which it must re-lend and it will also have to lend another $200,000 if a fall in the price level is to be avoided. The only possible "commercial" outlet, however, will be corporation E^2. But E^2 only wants $200,000 and therefore the bank is unable to maintain the desired increase in the money supply.

Suppose we allow the bank to make long term loans on fixed

capital. In Figure B the results will not change because there is full employment and no available investment outlets. However, if we allow the population to grow, or if we assume the existence of unemployment then the difficulty is temporarily overcome. But it is only overcome by assuming an immense increase in the rate of growth of employment, output and bank credit. Absolute output will increase in a very steep curve and at a rate of growth which probably cannot be maintained.

Another possible outlet is "personal" or installment loans to individuals by banks. In a society previously unaccustomed to such lending these afford temporary relief, but once repayment starts in large volume the difficulty of both re-lending what is repaid and maintaining a net injection reappears. Difficulties like this are usually dodged by the tacit assumption of a reserve of unemployment to permit extra lending. But in the model we have been using—and in the world supposed by the underconsumptionists—no such solution is possible.

INDEX

INDEX 115

Venus de Medici, 49n
Versailles, 51

Wages, 2, 14; contrast with profits, 18;
reduction and unemployment, 57,
58, 59; and prices, 64

War, and capital glut, 49n
Wright, D. McC., 54n, 58n, 63n, 88n,
89n, 90n, 98n

Yogis, 51